Brendan A Kilpatrick is a practicing architect working in London. He was born in County Tyrone, Northern Ireland, and studied Architecture in Liverpool. He is a Senior Partner at PRP in Central London, a firm which specialises in large-scale residential regeneration. Brendan is married to a Canadian furniture designer, Patricia, and has two sons.

This book is dedicated to my mother, Ita Kilpatrick,
who kept the memories alive.

B A Kilpatrick

ELEPHANT ON MAIN STREET

AUSTIN MACAULEY PUBLISHERS™

LONDON • CAMBRIDGE • NEW YORK • SHARJAH

A CIP catalogue record for this title is available from the British Library.

ISBN 9781528921473 (Paperback)
ISBN 9781528921480 (Hardback)
ISBN 9781528921497 (E-Book)

www.austinmacauley.com

First Published (2019)
Austin Macauley Publishers Ltd
25 Canada Square
Canary Wharf
London
E14 5LQ

Introduction

Stories are the lifeblood of the Irish. The old Gaelic tradition of the 'seanchaí' still survives somehow. This is the art of preserving the culture and history of the people through the spoken word, handed down from generation to generation. The people who still tell stories are revered and sought after, which is why older people are respected in Ireland whether they tell stories or not. They have lived the life and the knowledge they possess is important.

My family would grow around me and get even bigger after I left. My mother would tell stories about me which came across as tales, but she was telling the truth. They sounded like tales because they were a wee bit different and a wee bit incredible, especially when viewed through a modern prism, where children are coached and watched and worried over, long after they cease being children. My mother's stories were glimpses in time, told again and again as if the telling preserved the reality of what occurred as the 'seanchaithe' of old would have it. Her stories were about a young boy whose existence was brief but whose light shone brightly in the short time available, as if that child knew he had to pack as much into his life before it ceased. The stories preserve the memories. They also make it seem as if the boy never really left his family, that he was around as his siblings grew and his parents got older. This is the power of the spoken word.

That boy is me, Eamon, and this story is my story. I was born on October 9 1960 and died of leukaemia six and a half years later.

Chapter 1
Life

Leukaemia got me.

It was 1967. If I had been born 20 years later, I might have survived although my chances would still be slim. And if I had been born ten years after that, I probably would have been alright. Of course I didn't know all that at the time. I knew very little about it. I didn't know that pioneering research and treatment had just commenced in the United States that would be too late for me.

I knew about death though. Even though I missed The Troubles by a few years, death was never far from your doorstep in Ireland. It's part of life in fact, part of our DNA as they say now, especially in the North.

My big sister died suddenly as a baby just before I was born and this cast a shadow for a time over our family. Pneumonia killed her. Crept up behind her it did at Christmas of all times. She was buried at dusk in Pomeroy graveyard on Christmas Eve 1959, the snowflakes landing but not melting on her tiny white coffin as they lowered her into the ground. She was 10 months old. It was the last time Mum cried and she would have a few things to cry about in the course of her life. My dad said he'd go on the roads, like the travellers of old, to have his baby daughter back. I'm glad he didn't. I liked my Dad. We were a very close family. Dad fixed cars. He was also brilliant at fixing bikes and that was my chief mode of transport, apart from walking. That's the only choice you have when you are six, apart from the odd ride in a wheelbarrow. Hoverboards weren't available to me then.

My grandparents were dropping like flies as well. By the time my brother Brendan was born in 1963, only Granda

Canavan was left and he wasn't hangin' around either. He was cool though.

"Grandad – there's a bee on your lip!" Granda Canavan was dozing in a chair that had been brought outside so he could relax in the afternoon summer sun. He'd just finished a jam sandwich.

"He'll be alright lad – he's only after a wee bit of jam." Granda didn't flinch. The bee ate a bit of jam on his upper lip and flew off.

"Do you want a jam sandwich Eamon?" called my Aunty Sarah from the darkness inside the house.

"Naw, but the bees might!" I called back. Sarah was married to Mum's brother Sean, my granda's eldest son, who was nowhere to be seen. He must have been working in the fields.

We were in Greenhill. This is where Mum was born and grew up, in the gently rolling hills of Glencull, in the heartland of Tyrone, a few miles outside Ballygawley. The house looked like a Parish Priest's house, or a rich Protestant's house, with a double-bay window fronted façade and the front door in the middle, sitting on a commanding spot overlooking the Ballygawley-Omagh main road. Down by the roadside, it even had double cast iron entrance gates and fencing in the same style to either side, with the road sweeping up the side of the house to the rear yard where I now stood.

We knew the story about the son of the local landed gentry, Lord Brookborough, who had once tried to buy the ironwork off Granda but Granda refused to sell. The young aristocrat was amazed that Granda wasn't interested in a cash sale, no matter how much was offered, nor about who the offer was coming from.

"They're not for sale."

"Do you know who I am? I'm the son of Lord Brookborough!"

"Well lad, that's not your fault," Grandad had wryly responded.

The aristocracy retreated, defeated. The gates were safe.

It was also known in the family that Granda Canavan had been bequeathed the house by the British Government because of his heroics in the First World War. He'd been in the trenches

9

in the Somme where the Ulster regiments were unfortunate to find themselves and where they died in the thousands, Protestants and Catholics alike. Because he could handle horses, periodically he would take a team into no man's land to pick up the wounded and the dying. He volunteered once when the shells were landing thick and fast and no one would break cover for a medical rescue mission. The decision to go saved his life as a German shell landed in the trench after he had headed off to get the horses and took out five men around the spot where he had been standing.

He wasn't a big man but he was full of strength, even now in his older years. I often thought that only for his bravery and skill with animals there would be a different family living here – Protestants probably – and Mum and I wouldn't exist.

The house had a post office occupying the room behind the right hand bay window and was run by Aunty Sarah. That blew my mind. A post office in your living room, imagine that! You'd never run out of stamps and you could have as much family allowance money as you wanted.

Mum had one other brother, my Uncle Kieran. He was nowhere to be seen either but for different reasons. He was nowhere to be seen for several years now. My mum really missed him as they were close growing up.

Uncle Kieran had been a member of a nationalist insurgency group called Saor Uladh, which is Gaelic for Free Ulster and which had the aim of securing a united Ireland. He had taken part in the so called 'border campaign' in the early '50s. Saor Uladh was distinct from the old IRA, which continued to exist as an organisation after the turmoil of the Civil War had receded but which was less active now that most of the island of Ireland had secured independence. The greater part of Ulster remained under British rule.

The activities of Saor Uladh are not to be confused with what followed in The Troubles when the IRA effectively reformed and where the shackles were off on both sides of the conflict that followed. The border campaign was one of those periodic insurgencies that happened from time to time since the partition of the country and before that too, down through the centuries of English and then British Rule. The action was primarily against military and police installations and

10

infrastructure as opposed to deliberately killing people in the name of 'the cause' of re-uniting the island of Ireland. I knew little about what mayhem had been caused or my uncle's part in it but I knew that he had been on the run in County Monaghan, just across the border in the Republic, or the Free State as my Dad called it. The British could not reach you there as there was little or no cooperation between the Irish and British Governments in relation to police force collaboration or extradition. After lying low in Monaghan for a year or so, Uncle Kieran had made his way across the Atlantic, like so many Irishmen before him and was now in New York City. He had initially settled in The Bronx and worked as a carpenter. He met a woman from Crossmaglen, my Aunty Rose, and started a family of his own. I think he would have met me as a baby before he went into exile, maybe on a cross-border visit, but it was probably Mum that crossed the border to visit him and not the other way round. He would return much later in life to the six counties of Ulster within Northern Ireland but would keep a relatively low profile, as memories in Ireland are long.

The strong bond between Uncle Kieran and Mum would be passed onto their children and the cousins would become close despite three thousand miles of ocean between them. The bond would be strengthened by the tragic loss of Sean, Kieran's eldest boy who was born a year after me, but who was in the wrong place at the wrong time, high up in the South Tower, when the second plane hit the World Trade Centre in 2001.

I was watching my cousins, Barry and Kieran, who were close to my age, climbing on the metal link box attached to the back of an old grey Massey Ferguson tractor. Kieran had managed to perch himself on the tractor's curved metal seat and was preventing Barry from reaching the summit which he commanded. It was King of the Castle, agricultural style. The noise of their little tussle stirred Granda.

"Don't mind them Eamon. Take that football and see if you can kick it through that opening in the side of the byre," he said, opening his eyes from his dozing. They were completely nuts about football up here, boys, girls, cats, dogs, everybody was into Gaelic football.

"That's far too small Granda."

"It's big enough for a football Eamon."

"It is if you let the air out!" I replied, dismayed.

The Byre was a disused single storey cowshed at the back of the yard with a shallow, single pitched corrugated iron roof. Behind the byre were open fields laid out to pasture, with the odd Frisian cows lazily munching grass or chewing the cud, the odd tail swishing flies away nonchalantly. Uncle Sean owned the land as far as the brow of the hill, a couple of fields distant.

The opening in the side of the byre was a foot and a half square and about six feet off the ground with no glass or frame in it. This is the same opening that my yet to be born cousin, Peter Canavan, would practice kicking at, with both feet, as he commenced his journey to become the greatest Gaelic footballer the North had ever seen.

I picked up the ball.

"Steady yourself and pick the spot," he instructed. I started kicking the ball at the hole in the byre wall. My first shot was about three feet wide off the mark. Granda smiled as I scampered to retrieve the ball and wiped the last of the jam from his face.

I loved getting to Greenhill and Mum loved it too. There were twins in this house, just like there were in ours with my older brothers Kieran and Aidan who were five years older than me. In this house it was Stephen and Nuala. They were about three years old so there wasn't much crack out of them. I couldn't figure out how you could have a twin who was a girl. Something got seriously mixed up there. I wasn't sure how I'd deal with that if it had happened to me. Maybe just say nothing, keep your head down and hope for the best.

Mum came out with a chair and sat down beside her father.

"Well Daddy, any craic?" she asked.

"Well Ita, all's quiet."

"C'mon Daddy, it's never quiet around here. What have you been up to this week?"

"Well, I can tell you about a conversation I had the other day," he said.

"Go on," she replied excitedly, she loved her da's yarns.

"I was walkin' out the road and I was joined by Bob Wilson." We knew that Bob was a local Protestant farmer who was a friend of Grandad's.

"We got to talkin' about religion and the differences between the Protestant and Catholic faiths," he said.

"Bob was remarking on the importance we Catholics place on the Virgin Mary, even though she was just a woman. He reckoned that there wouldn't be much difference between the Virgin Mary and his own mother, both being good-hearted women."

"What did you say to that?" Mum asked, intrigued.

"I said to him – in fairness Bob, there mightn't be a big pile of difference between the two women but there's a hell of a difference between the two sons." Mum burst out laughing. I tried to figure out what I had just heard and then burst out laughing too. Grandad pointed to the byre and I resumed my target practice with the football.

Following a visit to Greenhill, we would also visit my mum's sisters Aunty Eileen in Gort, a few miles away, and Aunty Carmel in Garvaghy, which was also in the Ballygawley locality. Eileen was the second oldest in the family. She had four children at the time and would go on to have eight more. My Aunty Maureen was the eldest and had married an Englishman, a Protestant to boot and had gone to live in Bristol. I never clapped eyes on her and there was little contact, if any, between Maureen and the rest of the family in Ireland, unlike the relations in New York. The politics and religion of the time ensured separation from my English cousins, a separation which would take a generation to overcome.

There was a lot of contact with Carmel though, the youngest of the family. Mum had effectively raised Carmel in Greenhill as Carmel was a baby when my granny died and Mum was ten years of age, old enough to act like a Mum to Carmel. There were loads of other great aunts and second cousins knocking around this area too, like the Farrells, and Mum would do her best to call on them too for a visit.

But it was soon time to head back to Pomeroy. This was fine 'cos Dad had just got the coolest car in the world. It was a black MG Magnette with red leather seats and a Jackie Stewart steering wheel covered in black leather. In case you forgot it was an MG, it had big letters in the middle of the steering wheel to remind you. I suppose if you ran one of only two cars fixing businesses in town (the Garage as we called it), then you needed a cool set of wheels to advertise your trade. Dad always had cool cars.

We had one last call to make on our way home and Mum turned right out of the gates of Greenhill in the direction of Ballygawley. This was Mum's Uncle Packie's place. Uncle Packie was a Farrell. Farrell was his mother's name. Mum liked her uncle and Packie's daughter was one of Mum's favourite cousins and she said that you would always get a cup of tea and a chat and they had a kettle continually hanging in the fireplace. Mum said the Farrells all had music in them. The house was a small, detached, whitewashed building on the edge of the town, one of the prettiest towns in Tyrone. Woodsmoke and pipesmoke greeted us as we opened the door and walked into the little hallway. Packie was on his own, sitting in an old armchair by the fireplace with a pipe sticking out of a contented gob.

On the two-mile drive over to Ballygawley, Mum had opened the glovebox of the MG and handed me a little bunch of gold coins with chocolate inside. I was going to munch these with a cup of Uncle Packie's tea. As I was waiting for the tea, I noticed that Uncle Packie had a fiddle hanging on the wall opposite the fireplace. It looked beautiful and I wanted it. I got out my gold coins.

"Play a tune on the fiddle for us, Uncle Packie?"

Uncle Packie ignored me and carried on chatting to Mum. I persisted, "C'mon, Uncle Packie. Get the fiddle down!"

Uncle Packie stoked the fire and continued to ignore me and now I was getting frustrated.

"I'll buy it off you," I said. I rattled a few of my gold coins together to get his attention. My great-uncle still paid me no heed. I needed to get out of here. This was a waste of time.

"You won't play it. You won't sell it. What good is it to you?" And at that, I nodded to Mum and we were out of there. She totally got my drift. That was the last time I saw him.

The MG made short work of the roller-coaster hills and corners of the 16-mile journey back home. Mum knew the road so well she handled the blind corners and the bumps like a professional driver. It's a good job my wee brother Brendan wasn't with us or he'd have been boking all over the place. He was a disaster with car sickness and you couldn't take him anywhere.

We were home in no time.

Our house was pretty cool too.

I always thought it had been built especially for me because Kieran and Aidan had lived in Cookstown for a while when they were wee babies and this house was only completed just before I was born. When I got mad at them, I'd tell them that they weren't even proper Pomeroy men. They didn't like that one bit.

The house was detached, covered in white dash with painted concrete windowsills and metal windows painted light blue. It had a red tile roof from which protruded a chimney, also rendered like the walls with two red clay chimney pots with galvanised wire guards to stop birds making nests. The living room window and main bedroom window above commanded the centre of the dwelling facing south. The house had a garage with an up-and-over timber boarded door which was to the left of the house, but connected. The garage door was mostly kept shut so it could act as our goal when we played soccer and we pretended to be George Best. The front drive was big enough for three or four to play football into one goal or you could use the lawn, which was a bit bigger than the drive but you had the advantage of the privet hedge as your goal.

To the side of the garage was a field which we owned with Connolly's garage beyond, a large shed of a building where John Connolly had a car repair business and petrol pumps on the forecourt. Mum and Dad planted spuds in this field and put us to work when it was time to harvest the potato crop or store them for the winter. Not that we minded. Mum had a unique ability to get us all working, including some of the neighbours' children, while having us all thinking that we were havin' the time of our lives which, I suppose, we were.

Even though the house had only three bedrooms, it looked massive to me. It was situated in the centre of Pomeroy, exactly halfway between the 'old town' and the new Council housing estates, Keeragh and Park View, which had just been built. These were terraces of two storey houses and the odd bungalow, all built in a simple architectural style with pebble dash render and dark concrete tile roofs. Keeragh was the smaller of the two estates, laid out in a crescent overlooking a central green with a road around it. The green was great for playing soccer matches, with schoolbags or upright sticks for goalposts, but you needed to watch out and mind where you fell because nobody ever picked up dog poo in those days.

Park View was the larger and more recent estate. It was further west than Keeragh and this estate finished the western developed edge of the village. Beyond that was farmland and beyond that again was the bogland near the Black Lough and the White Lough where you could dig turf for your fire to your heart's content.

There were about fifty houses between the two estates. They were populated mainly by Catholics although there were a few Protestant families living in Keeragh. Just behind Keeragh was Pomeroy's Gaelic football pitch and clubhouse, Plunkett Park, where Pomeroy Plunketts played. The club was named after Joseph Plunkett, one of the heroes of the 1916 Easter Rising, executed shortly afterwards by the British. Born in Dublin, he was the youngest signatory to the Proclamation of Independence but was also the chief military strategist of the Rising.

The football pitch was kind of diagonally opposite our property so there would be no excuse for poor footballers coming out of our house.

The Plunketts played an important part in the life of the family and the club at the heart of the community. Dad was very active at club and county level and all of my brothers would play football for the The Plunketts. My baby brother Enda and as yet unborn brother Niall would go on to captain the senior squad and Enda would go even further to become the first Pomeroy man to captain the senior Gaelic football Tyrone county team. He would even play in an All-Ireland final. No excuse at all.

The southern flank of the football pitch gave way, after a few yards, to the steep slopes descending to the Gortnagarn River, a fast flowing stream which followed in part the line of the Great Northern Railway, the trains of which had ceased snaking their way through the valley just a year before. The view from here was probably the best in the village, east and west, up and down the Gortnagarn Valley, an uninterrupted vista of wild green countryside, tamed in parts by farming, from The Bonn and beyond to the east to Sluggan to the west. At night you could see the twinkling lights of Dungannon, some ten miles distant to the east.

To the immediate west of our house was a stand of trees and bushes, which we called The Forest, a wooded area within the parochial grounds which was probably the only bit of undeveloped natural landscape within the town, the rest given over to either buildings or agriculture. Beyond the Forest was the Parochial House. Now that was a proper priest's house. It was situated on higher ground, about twelve feet above the main road. It was about sixty years old and was built in a simple Irish classical way, with double height bay windows on the front elevation with their own little pitched roofs and decorative finials on the roof ridges and stone framing around the timber sash windows. The storey heights were much bigger than normal houses in the village and there was a large stained circular glass window with stone tracery above the central entrance door to remind you that there was a priest hereabouts. The double entrance door was white painted with two equal door leaves and big black painted cast iron door handles and hinges opening into a little tiled porch. The inside door of the porch had more stained glass in it which partially concealed the view into the hallway beyond. I liked looking through the red bits of glass to see if I could spot anyone inside, all in red. The front of the house looked directly onto the eastern flank of the Church of the Assumption, the principal Catholic Church of the parish of Pomeroy, about 50 yards in front, as if to keep an eye on it.

This is a magnificent stone-built building in a simple Roman style and a cruciform plan. It has very narrow but high stained glass windows, finished with cut stone surrounds and arched window heads. The entrance gable, which faces south looking out towards Gortnagarn, is topped with a simple bell tower below which is a large rose window, also in stained glass with stone tracery, lighting the gallery of the interior.

A footpath followed a gentle slope from the Parochial House down to the chapel and connected with the church grounds at the northeast corner, just to the rear of the chapel. If you turned left now another wider path took you up a slight incline to the graveyard with a small field separating it from the chapel. That field would one day become the spill-over graveyard.

Just as you approached the intersection of these two paths, on the left hand side was an earth bank which was about a foot higher than I was tall. It was probably man-made from the excavations of the church foundations all those years before but there were bushes growing out of the top of it now. I had noticed little ridges in the bank about a foot below its top which were like little earthen shelves. You could put your hand into these ridges up to your wrist. This is where I hid my savings, my pennies, thrupenny bits, shillings and the odd sixpence. It was a piggy-bank in a bank. No one would ever rob it 'cos they would never know it was there. After all, who would leave money in a ditch? Plus it was in church grounds so it would have angels guarding it too. It was safer than Fort Knox.

Father McDermott was the Parish Priest and spent most of his time in the Parochial House in the first room on the right as you entered the building. He was the oldest person I had ever seen, grey hairs growing out of his ears and everything, but he hadn't lost his marbles and he didn't smell or anything. He couldn't move much outside his home without the help of a wheelchair.

The room he occupied was quite formal and old-fashioned with holy looking wallpaper and proper carpet. The room had two windows, one looking east towards the chapel and one looking north towards the Sperrins. The float glass of the windows in his room distorted the countryside when you put your eye close to the pane as there were little imperfections in the glass. *This must be glass getting old and wrinkly*, I thought. Father McDermott had a luxurious wing-back armchair close to the fireplace. In the corner between the front-facing window and the fireplace was a big dresser, close enough to his chair for him to reach. He had a secret stash of Fry's Chocolate Cream in one of the drawers and would always give me a piece when I visited. He got mad at Kathleen once when she came back from the shops with the wrong chocolate.

Pride of place on the wooden mantelpiece above the fireplace was perched a life-size statue of a scary black raven with a lethal looking beak and shiny black obsidian eyes. It looked like it was just pretending to be dead so I would keep checking to see if it moved. You wouldn't see me for dust if it did.

The housekeeper, Kathleen, always had an expression of perpetual worry on her face and had a walk like she was in a hurry all the time, but she had a heart of gold and would have done anything for us. She would press a homemade bun into my hand every time she saw me, which wasn't great 'cos she couldn't bake to save her life and if she managed to get kissing you on the side of the cheek, she'd leave a big slobbery wet leftover. She would give you Rich Tea biscuits which were literally at the bottom of the biscuit food-chain as far as I was concerned, with no chocolate on it or anything. But Mum made sure we'd eat the bun and eat the dry biscuit and not wipe your cheek until Kathleen looked away.

Mum would often drop us here when she had to go somewhere or if she was off having babies or something. They didn't have a larder like us but they had a scullery which wasn't the same thing to my mind. It opened off the room where Kathleen spent most of her time and had a big yellow range which kept the room toasty. We stayed and played in this room when Kathleen was looking after us. I wasn't one for hanging around though. I spent loads of time there exploring the dark rooms of the main house and it's outhouses to the rear.

The outhouses formed the enclosure to the yard. These were old farm buildings and stables. Inside these structures, the smell of whitewash was overpowering. One of the rooms was an old external toilet or privy as the English would call it, with a wooden seat and two circular holes side by side and no sign of a cistern. Toilets side by side! What on earth were they thinking about? The larger outhouse rooms were like something out of Dr Who with ancient bits of furniture from the Chapel and statues of everyone who came out at Christmas. Mary, Joseph, wise men, shepherds and sheep and an ass (that's what they call donkeys in the Bible) all stared at me out of the gloomy damp dank atmosphere. They were all huddled together, not like I'd seen them before, carefully making moves around the manger at the front of the chapel around Christmas time. The manger – it was there, it even had hay in it, but there was no sign of the wee Baby Jesus. So I started investigating his disappearance, true detective style. I started searching the building. The closer I looked for evidence, the more I noticed that the statues had all developed some sort of deformity – well by deformity I mean bits of ears or noses or fingers missing, chipped off somehow, like King Herod had got to them in advance. It looked like these boys had done their tour of duty and were now held in reserve, waiting for the statue doctor to pay them a visit and their chance to break back into the limelight.

But the disappearance of the Baby Jesus troubled me most. Then I remembered.

Father McDermott had told us that the Devil lived in another outhouse. He had even showed it to us once and it was the first and last time I ever looked at it. It had scared the life out of us. The place where the Devil lived was in a stable-like building attached to the main house, which formed most of one side of the yard enclosure on the northern side. Part of the long building was given over to a small square space close to the entrance gate to the yard. The interior was dimly lit by a dusty window close to the timber-boarded entrance door. Father McDermott had moved a big wooden cover on the earthen floor and told us to stand back. This was me and my wee brother Brendan. He was only three so he didn't know what day of the week it was. The old priest grabbed me by the arm and told me to grab Brendan's arm to keep him behind me.

He edged us closer.

The wooden cover had concealed a perfectly circular hole in the floor of the outhouse, defined by a cut stone surround. He picked up a large pebble from the floor and reaching out a long bony hand, dropped in into the hole. We waited to hear it hit the bottom. We waited and waited. We heard nothing.

"See?" said Father McDermott. "That's the drop to Hell and that's where the Devil lives!"

I couldn't get out of there quick enough. Even Brendan knew he needed to be gone and he didn't have a clue.

So that's where my first piece of detective work ended. The Devil had somehow managed to get a hold of the wee Baby Jesus but there was no way I was rescuing him. I was only six. What could I do?

I learned later that the hole was the old well for the big house, but I had no way of figuring that out 'cos we had running water in our house and what the hell was a well, if not Hell?

Leukaemia is a type of blood cancer that affects your blood cells, usually white blood cells. The word 'leukaemia' comes from the Greek word for 'white blood'. White blood cells are an important part of your immune system that fight infection. White blood cells like these are made within the marrow of you bones which is where the cancer usually starts.

When I developed leukaemia, I had built up large numbers of abnormal blood cells, which took over the bone marrow and spilled over out into my bloodstream. They were immature structures known as lymphoblasts. These are primitive-looking globules which began to crowd out my healthy blood cells. As they started to course through my body, these cancerous blobs began to accumulate and take over, literally causing my blood to grow pale.

White blood cells protect your body from invasion by bacteria, viruses, and fungi, as well as from abnormal cells and other foreign substances. In leukaemia, white blood cells don't function like normal white blood cells. They can divide too quickly and eventually crowd out normal cells.

Whilst mostly produced in your bone marrow, certain types of white blood cells are also produced in the lymph nodes, spleen, and thymus gland. Once formed, they circulate throughout your body in your blood and lymph, concentrating in the lymph nodes and spleen.

Chapter 2
Village

Pomeroy was brilliant.

"The highest village in Northern Ireland," my dad would proudly proclaim. Pomeroy had nine pubs, three churches, ten shops, two schools (one protestant, one catholic), two butchers (one protestant, one catholic), a fire station, a post office, a police station, a handball alley, a Forestry School, an Orange Hall, a county-standard Gaelic football pitch and there was a New Hall soon to be under construction for concerts and the showbands to come, like Big Tom and the Mainliners and Brian Coll and the Buckeroos. Pomeroy would even have its own show band a few years later with its country and western music star, Philomena Begley and the Country Flavour. Philomena was a friend of Mum's which was pretty cool. The village had a railway station too, but it had recently closed for good. There used to be a courthouse but it was closed now too. The village even had an accordion band that would come out on special occasions and big Gaelic football matches.

The old part of the town was formed around an old fashioned square with the Church of Ireland church in the middle. Why the square was called The Diamond, God only knows 'cos there was nothing diamond-shaped about it. It was square. And God must have known why there was a Protestant church dating from 1877 smack bang in the middle of a Catholic town. Not that I ever saw anyone using it, not a sinner. It just sat there in stony silence while the life of the village pulsated around it.

All of the buildings overlooking The Diamond were run by, or lived in by Catholics. The Catholic curate of the parish, Father McKeown, and his housekeeper Sheila even lived on the east side of the Diamond directly overlooking the Protestant

Church. The main street, funnily enough known as Main Street, formed the principal edge of The Diamond heading east-west through the town. There was only one road heading south out of town and that was at the start of Main Street, just before the Police Station and this wound its way down and past the old Railway Station where it bridged the now disused railway line. No other roads were built on the south side of town because of the steepness of the terrain. The village was literally perched on a hillside, the head of Main Street being the summit.

To those who disliked Pomeroy, you were a prisoner of both geography and history.

The history got you if you were a Catholic because you were almost certainly the descendants of the dispossessed, eking out an existence on the poorest land around the area. The bog-free arable land was in the hands of the Protestant ascendency since the early 1600s when the Plantation of Ulster occurred following the final defeat by Crown forces of the old Celtic Chieftain order. Hugh O'Neill, the last of that order in Tyrone and the effective leader of the Irish resistance, had held the north against successive English incursions, keeping at bay the ascendant power of Queen Elizabeth I. However, he could not battle un-aided forever. After the final defeat, O'Neill and his clansmen and his supporting Celtic noblemen from across the north fled Ireland forever. A thousand years of the way things were done in the ancient pre-Christian province of Ulster changed almost overnight. The English forces moved north and initially inherited a wasteland, deprived and debilitated from decades of keeping superior forces at bay.

The English Government had the Protestant planters moved in, coming principally from Scotland, East Lothian, Lanarkshire and Midlothian to this part of the province. It was the English method for taking control for good. Other planters were Crown servants who were resident in Ireland. The planters gradually became Irish over the generations, much as the Normans had done eight hundred years before, but unlike the Normans, they didn't know they had changed. They spoke like us and didn't look too dissimilar from us. They just didn't realise they were Irish now and would remain confused for generations. Even two generations after me, a lot of them would still be confused.

The geography got you too if you didn't like the place.

You were in the middle of nowhere, almost equidistant between the three principal towns of Tyrone, Omagh – the County Town – Cookstown and Dungannon, all much larger than Pomeroy. Belfast was 55 miles away, three hours' drive in the mid-60s because it was before the construction of the M1 motorway linking Dungannon swiftly to the capital of Northern Ireland. It would be a couple more years before it reached Dungannon in 1968.

The geography of the place would play its part in The Troubles, yet to come, too. The police station at the foot of the town would be transformed into one of the most fortified, bombproof barracks buildings in Northern Ireland. It needed to be fortified as there would be a number of audacious attacks on the compound in the years ahead. For several years, the roads would not be safe to be travelled on by the security forces and all traffic to and from the barracks by army personnel would be by helicopter. This area of Tyrone was not quite the 'bandit country' that South Armagh would become, but it wasn't far off.

If you liked Pomeroy, you were King of the Hill. All roads led from Pomeroy in all directions and you were smack bang in the middle of everywhere, like the bullseye on an Ulster dartboard, able to go north, south, east or west and already be halfway on your journey to your final destination. You would never get flooded out of your home no matter how rainy it got because all the water would drain away. On top of that, you had commanding views of the countryside all around, a majestic half-wild landscape of hills and valleys and wind-blown trees and no other settlements in sight. It is a landscape that no one living there truly appreciates because it was always there and you don't recognise beauty if you've never seen ugliness.

I liked it so I suppose that made me King of the Hill, or at least some kind of Prince.

At the head of Main Street was my Dad's garage and shop – well technically it was Dad's and Uncle Jim's. Dad ran the garage and Jim the hardware store. They called it the upper shop because there was another Kilpatrick store, a newsagent and small grocer's which they called the Lower Shop, and the house behind and above the shop where Dad had grown up. It was on Main Street overlooking The Diamond. Main Street got really steep going downhill towards the police station at the foot of the town. This was a perfect launch pad for the King of the Hill go-cart races that would come to the village decades later.

Some Protestants lived around the foot of the town close to the police station, as if for protection. Not that there was trouble between the two sides of the community. It was before The Troubles and everyone got on pretty well. Even around the 12th of July, when the Orange bands came out in force, Catholics would also come out to see the parades and join in the celebrations. My youngest brothers would find this amazing as The Troubles gradually shaped their world view and Orangemen became bogeymen as The Troubles intensified.

At the rear of The Diamond, another street headed steeply downhill going directly north. It was easy to remember the name of this street as it was called Back Street. I wondered who thought of that. Just to confuse things, it was also called North Street. A quarter of the way down Back Street was a turning into Lucy Street. This ran parallel with Main Street until it reached a road called Limehill. This was the second of the two roads heading north out of town in the direction of the Sperrin Mountains, winding its way down through The Sweeps before straightening out and heading for the hills. The Catholic primary school lay 100 yards further back behind Limehill. I never found out who Lucy was and why she was important enough to have one of Pomeroy's precious few roads named after her.

Treanor's Terrace was practically a pedestrian-only street which linked Lucy Street back to Main Street coming out behind the Arch Tavern. When you ran down it towards Lucy Street you could hear the echo of the soles of your gutties bouncing off the close confined walls on either side making an odd bouncy, twangy sound. Just where it came out onto Main Street was an ancient stone jutting out into the footpath. It was about two feet high, with the building on this side of the street built around and on top of it leaving the stone in place. Its edges were perfectly rounded from years of old men sitting on it, for it was a perfect seat, watching the world go by on Main Street.

On the other side of Treanor's terrace facing Main Street was the O'Neill residence where my granny, Ellen O'Neill, had lived. I had taken it for granated that Grandma was a direct descendant of the great Hugh O'Neill so I could justifiably call myself a prince of the house O'Neill. Ellen had married my grandad Jimmy Kilpatrick and had died in the late fifties but it was the O'Neills who had given Dad the land to build his house in Pomeroy on Cavanakeeran Road. It was his mother, Ellen, making sure that he came back to the village he grew up in when it looked like he might have settled with his new young family in Cookstown.

The site of the first Catholic Church built in Pomeroy and its ancient graveyard was next to the Upper Shop. The church was long gone but in its place was a rough stone structure with arched portals on either side flanking a central corbelled recess which housed a white statue of the Virgin Mary. She was standing guard about halfway up and sheltered by the corbelling. This structure was called The Grotto. My older twin brothers, Kieran and Aidan, had their photograph taken here at the time of their First Holy Communion three years before, kneeling on the step, one on either side, looking up at the Virgin with their hands together as if in prayer and perfectly angelic. As if! I wondered if the Virgin Mary was sniggering at them when they had pulled that one.

The graveyard behind The Grotto was the scariest place in Pomeroy at Halloween, all overgrown, with gravestones so old and moss covered you couldn't read them. Some of the graves had stone covers and a couple of these were cracked so you see the darkness beneath which always freaked us out. We'd be sure to pay a visit well before midnight each Halloween to scare the life out of ourselves, always making sure we got the hell out before the clock struck twelve when the graves opened at the end of All Hallows Eve and the dead souls started walking.

Funnily enough, the Protestants didn't come out at Halloween. They came out five nights later to celebrate Guy Fawkes Night but the Catholics stayed in that evening. Halloween was much more fun. Dad's sister would come and make us big tall false faces out of wallpaper and a paint set, like a big scary Abraham Lincoln hat with holes cut out for your eyes and mouth. We'd dress up in our false faces, go knocking on doors, run away and have water balloon fights on The Diamond. The bigger boys took the gates to farmers' fields off their hinges and turned signposts the wrong way round.

At home, we had apples bobbing in basins of water, apples on string hanging from the door jamb and home-made toffee apples. I usually skipped the first of these as it was too much like hard work and you needed a supergob to grab the apples with your teeth. Mum would also put coins wrapped in tinfoil inside her apple pies so the pies didn't last long. Then there were the fireworks – sparklers, squibs, Catherine Wheels and rockets. Within five years, fireworks would be banned for thirty years at the outset of The Troubles. They would let sparklers escape the ban but you couldn't do much with a sparkler at the best of times.

The fact that there were nine pubs meant that nearly every other house was a pub. I would be in and out of all of them, Peter Daly's, The Arch Tavern owned by ole Micky Nugent, Al Lagan's Dew Drop Inn, the one at the back of The Diamond called Donnelly's and Lagan's other pub which was the one with the Ghost in the Bottle. A priest had put the ghost in there and sealed it with a cork following a series of scary episodes years before. The bottle was built into the wall and was not to be touched, ever, and it wasn't. It's still there, entombed in the wall. It is the only haunted house in the village.

The only pub I didn't really go into was Heatherington's 'cos Billy Heatherington didn't seem to like kids much and the men in there didn't seem very happy. There was one only Protestant pub, Ernie Stewart's bar, called The Balmoral Arms and I was in there more than I was in Billy's. Ernie Stewart and my Uncle Sean had started Pomeroy's volunteer fire service in the '50s, stationed in a large shed behind Main Street.

Three churches and nine pubs, one of them with a ghost. You could tell what was important to the people of Pomeroy.

Years later, Brendan made a Monopoly board of Pomeroy using as a base the board from a 007 Thunderball game that the brothers had stopped playing. He used Monopoly money from the real Monopoly game but made up the Chance and Community Chest cards. You could get fined for stealing a sheep or smuggling stuff across the border or being caught with a poteen still and stuff like that. But he would struggle with the street names as there weren't too many before you hit open countryside and who'd want to put a hotel on Carrickmore Road?

Peter Daly's pub probably had the best spot on The Diamond. Facing east overlooking the Church, you could sit outside on a bench or the low windowsills on either side of the pub entrance and watch the world go by. The pub's interior was quite simple, one room with the bar on your right as you entered and a square shaped room to the left with about five tables and chairs dotted around haphazardly. I went in early one day and Peter was standing behind the bar drying a glass. The double doors were open and the smell of slightly stale beer and pipe-smoke greeted me as I entered.

Peter was a bull of a man with Brillo Pad hair and a thick neck and, like all publicans in the village, he wore a jumper under his suit. It was like a uniform. He had a great love for traditional Irish music and he had a band playing in the pub at least once a week. I climbed up onto a big stool at the bar. It was just past noon and the pub was beginning to fill up.

"Would you take a drink Eamon?"

"I will if you give it to me in a man's glass."

Peter reached for a short glass, testing me.

"Ach c'mon now Peter!" Peter put the short glass down and poured my coke into a pint glass.

On the bar stood a solitary bottle of whiskey with an optic instead of a bottle cap or a cork. POWERS IRISH WHISKEY and GOLD LABEL in smaller letters in case you were colour blind because the triangular label was golden-coloured. The dark amber liquid was from County Cork. It said on the bottle that it was established in 1791, about 40 years before the potato famine. It wouldn't have been much use to the hungry. Peter grabbed the bottle and fixed it upside down to a high shelf in between a bottle of Jameson and a bottle of Bushmills.

In the corner of the room sat John Loughran, the blind fiddler. He wasn't fiddling now though. Sitting beside him was Hughie McErlane. Hughie was nursing a glass of stout with a whiskey chaser. John wasn't a drinker and he had what looked like a glass of red lemonade in front of him. John's fiddle case was on the seat beside him, ready for action. I'd heard it said that he wasn't the best fiddler in Ireland, but he was the only blind fiddler that we knew, so he was definitely the best blind fiddler in Ireland and he was from Pomeroy and here he was in Daly's pub.

"How's it going John?" I called over.

"Is that young Kilpatrick?" He winced over at me from behind his dark glasses.

"Aye, Eddie's lad." I pre-empted the perennial question – was I Eddie's lad or his brother Sean's lad – cos there was loads of lads in both families and people always had to know which family it was you were from for some reason.

"Stay off the stout!" Hughie called to me.

"It'll be twelve years before I touch that stuff and the Coke tastes better anyhow."

"Coke better than Guinness? That's total bollox but I'll raise a glass to you all the same," responded Hughie, lifting his glass of stout, which was almost empty. He must have been in here since the pub opened by the sound of him.

Hughie was the village coffin maker and was almost as colourful a local character as John Loughran. He was fond of the drink and some said he would sleep in one of his coffins at night, like Dracula or something, after he'd been on the sauce.

It was the Fair Day in Pomeroy, the second Tuesday of the month and I was off school as it was the Easter holidays. I'd spent the morning mooching around the sales-yard behind the houses at the head of the town. That was where cattle were bought and sold. Farmers came from miles around, Protestant and Catholic alike, to trade and deal. It was great fun. The smell of the animals in close confinement drowned out the smell of the farmers themselves. They all dressed the same, like Al Beggs but with wellys and one or two of them carried blackthorn sticks to help guide their beasts. The loud drone of the auctioneer commanded everything. I hadn't a clue what he was saying but the farmers seemed to know. Animals were sold in quick succession and the odd farmer who'd lost out on a purchase would take off his peaked cap and rub his brow in frustration.

Peter Rafferty, better known as Petey Dick, a farmer from Gortnagarn, lifted me onto his shoulders for a better view. The cows and bulls were paraded into a circular compound with walls taller than me in the middle of the enclosure. The roof covering was corrugated iron sheets supported by small girders resting on rusty steel columns. Bulls were led by a rope tied through a ring in their nose. *How did they get the ring in there without the bull making mincemeat out of you?* I wondered. The bulls snorted and wheezed and looked a bit hacked off. I was glad I was on Petey Dick's shoulders.

In between the auctioneer's monotone delivery, little groups of farmers in twos and threes and fours joined in deep conversations. This is where they met and learned from each other I supposed. They were in the same business and there was no thought of religious difference. They would speak about Massey Fergusons and John Deeres and about who was the best at taking in the silage in the months to come. This is where the farmers improved themselves.

The Fair Day also brought loads of traders who set up market stalls on The Diamond. You could buy everything you needed from oranges to galvanised buckets, from black pudding to herring. One of the stalls had spuds from Dublin. It was class.

Now, with the cattle trading over, the pubs were filling up with farmers celebrating a good morning's dealing and the many punters who had come in from the surrounding countryside to buy from the stalls and maybe have a drink. The Diamond was packed with covered stalls, set up cheek by jowl with every bit of space taken, and people you would never usually see would appear in town for the day.

This was Pomeroy at its busiest.

The causes of leukaemia are not known although a number of factors have been identified which may increase your risk of contracting the disease. This includes a family history of leukaemia, smoking, genetic disorders or blood disorders or exposure to hazardous chemicals or radiation.

There had been no prior instances of leukaemia in my family. I was the first and hopefully the last.

The long-term outlook and prognosis for people who have leukaemia depends on the type of cancer they have and their stage at diagnosis. The sooner leukaemia is diagnosed and the faster it's treated, the better the chance of recovery. Some factors, like older age, past history of blood disorders, and chromosome mutations, can negatively affect your prognosis.

The overall mortality rate for leukaemia has been falling about 1 percent each year for the past decade.

Chapter 3
Roaming

I loved wandering all over the place to visit people. Some people called it 'going on your ceilidh' from the Gaelic word for a party or a gathering and I would travel near and far.

Some days I'd walk for miles – outside the village to visit friends of Dad or his customers. I would get one of my classmates to throw my schoolbag into our garage at the side of the house after school and I would head out on my travels. I would seek out people who had something to say and had a bit of craic about them or could tell a good story about the old days. Young or old, near or far, it didn't matter. It made no difference to me.

Connolly's next door was easy to visit, usually by cutting through the back fields. Kitty Connolly had spent some time in America and had a touch the Yank about her accent plus she used a dead chicken wing for a duster which I though was brilliant.

The McAleers who made concrete blocks and Donnellys down the Dungannon Road both had houses which were situated well outside the village and these were two of my favourites.

One Saturday, I headed eastwards out of the village and called down to see John-Joe Donnelly singing to myself a version of 'The Wanderer' as I went.

"I'm the type of guy that likes to roam around,

I pick 'em and I choose 'em and I roam from town to town…"

I had to change the lyrics a bit 'cos the singer went on a bit too much about kissing and squeezing girls. I had no time for that sort of malarkey.

John-Joe owned the only furniture shop in town and he would let me have the run of the place, up and down the aisles of furniture, crawling under dinner tables and bed frames and hiding in wardrobes and sideboards. Today, I was in time for one of John-Joe's furniture runs.

John-Joe had set about making a fry for a late breakfast as I came into the kitchen.

"Well Eamon, do you want a bite to eat?"

"That would be great, thanks John-Joe," I replied.

He got out a large blue willow pattern plate and put all the bacon and sausage and black pudding and white pudding onto it. He grabbed a small white plate and set the plate on the table in front of me and sat down beside me with the big plate of food in front of him. He put a single sausage and a single piece of bacon onto my plate. I looked at my plate and then looked at John-Joe's plate and looked at mine again.

"Ach now John-Joe!" I declared.

He had been awaiting my indignant reaction and a broad grin flashed across his face. He handed me a proper sized plate and equalised the rations. We tucked in contentedly and talked about the day's business in the shop.

"You've got the quere appetite Eamon."

"So do you John-Joe."

"Do you fancy a trip down to the border?" he asked.

"I think I can squeeze that into my schedule," I replied. "Which bit of the border?"

"Newry, South Armagh," he replied. I'd been close to there before as we had relatives on my dad's side of the family living in Crossmaglen, which would become a border hotspot during The Troubles.

We made good time on our drive to Newry in John-Joe's big van. Our destination took us close to the customs checkpoint on the border. A slow trickle of traffic was coming and going in both directions. In time, this would be one of the most fortified border crossing points in Europe, outside Checkpoint Charlie.

"One day you'll be able to drive straight across with no bother from the police or customs officials on either side," said John-Joe.

"When will that be?" I asked.

"Not in my lifetime, but hopefully in yours, when people on this island see sense."

"We are in the Gap of the North," said John-Joe as we drove along. I looked out at the grey tarmac straight ahead and noticed that the land started to slope upwards on either side of the road and quickly became heavily wooded.

"This is where Hugh O'Neill stopped the advancing English soldiers. He would attack them in short bursts, guerrilla style and then retreat and that's how he kept the invaders out of Ulster."

My mind drifted back more than three and a half centuries as I tried to picture what O'Neill's men would have looked like coming screaming out of the trees to attack the foreign soldiers.

John-Joe had a drop-off to do in Warrenpoint and that was the return point of the trip. He had me back home before six o'clock and before I was missed by Mum.

I also spent a lot of time in Beggs's, just up the road from our house. Brendan Beggs had a big family and they were all friendly, with children both older and younger than me. Kieran Beggs was around my age. One afternoon after school I was headin' out through the front door and found that Dad was blocking my way.

"Where are you off to?" he asked.

"Beggs's."

"You are practically living there. If you think that much of the Beggses why don't you take your schoolbag with you and stay there?" he remarked.

I took two steps back and grabbed the bag from where I'd discarded it minutes earlier.

"Right-o," I said and squeezed past him on my way out.

"You'll get a bizzer along the lug," I knew Dad's threat to give me a thick ear was an idle one as I could feel his eyes on my back and I knew he was smirking.

One of the easiest visits was my Uncle Sean's, which was 100 yards up the road, opposite Keeragh, the new housing estate. The house was an old farmhouse, set back from the road on an incline with a medium height wall and pillars defining the opening into the neat tarmac covered front yard. The entrance walls to the yard curved back just like ours but the walls and pillars were taller. A bus stop was positioned just beside this entrance so schoolchildren heading into the big schools in Dungannon and the Convent school in Donaghmore would hang around these walls to Uncle Sean's place each school-day morning. There was no bus shelter so if it rained you got wet.

The house was on the left and to the right an untidy lane, littered with discarded bits of farm machinery, led the way to the farm buildings and fields beyond. Uncle Sean had a sizeable dairy farm and had a big milking shed behind the house. My uncle's orange Volkswagen Camper Van with a sticky-up roof was parked in front of the house. He always had one of those knocking around for trips to Donegal. Uncle Sean had married Aine, a woman who was born and bred in Rannafast, in the Gaeltacht area of Donegal. Gaelic was her first language so you had to have your wits about you when she addressed you as she was doing her best to single-handedly keep the old language alive.

"Ca é mar atá tú, a Eamoinn?" she asked as I crossed the threshold.

"Tá me go maith," I replied. That's almost as far as we had been taught of our native language at school. Aunty Aine seemed to know when to leave well enough alone and wouldn't press us too much with the Gaelic, apart from getting us to count to ten, of course. Before she even asked I started counting, just to reassure her.

"A haon, a dó, a trí a ceathair, a cúig, a sé, a seacht…"

"Buachaill maith deas!" She smiled at me. That meant I was a good boy.

She was sitting near the big yellow range in the kitchen on a rocking chair, bags of wool around her. A radio on the shelf near the range was switched on and was just about audible with Elvis Presley singing Jailhouse Rock. There was a smell of boiled cabbage in the room.

Aine was sitting knitting. She was always knitting. She looked older than her years because she dressed like it was 100 years ago, in dark Donegal clothes. Her dark curly hair had more grey than dark in it and the wrinkles were about the corners of her eyes, helping her to smile more often than a lot of people. Her daughter Brid was messing with some balls of wool on the floor. She was almost the exact same age as our

Brendan and clearly almost equally clueless at this stage of the game, if a few balls of wool could keep her entertained.

"What are you knitting?"

"I'm knitting an Aran sweater for you Eamon. Geansaí bán." She couldn't help herself. The Gaelic for white jumper was easy for me to translate as both words were in common usage in English in the north, especially geansaí, the word for jumper. Ban was used a lot too within names of people and places. The Catholic butcher in the village was called Micky Ban which meant White Micky. I had no idea why he was called that. He was no whiter than the next man.

Aine returned to English.

"What are you up to today young man?" Her Donegal brogue made her sound like she had honey on her tongue, rich and thick, and it must have been Scottish honey 'cos I swear I could detect a faint hint from our Celtic cousins across the Irish Sea.

"Why do you sound Scottish Aunty Aine – kind of?"

She looked surprised then smiled.

"Well, there were a lot of workers travelling between Donegal and Scotland in the old days, across the top of Ireland, doing seasonal work and I suppose there was a fair bit of inter-marrying." *Workers* – the way she said it, it could have come straight out of the Highlands of Scotland.

"Good job you married a proper Irishman," I declared.

"Well he's Irish alright! And he's fairly proper too!"

There was no doubt about that. Sean was so Irish he had become fluent in the old language and most of his children would become fluent too. And he was proper because he didn't drink. He was a 'Pioneer' with a pin he wore on his jacket lapel to declare to the countryside how proper he was, not drinking and all. I thought it was an odd word to choose for this abstentionist movement. Pioneer to me conjured up images of Davy Crockett and Wild Bill Hickock and people like that exploring new trails through the Rockies and fighting bears and things. I suppose Pioneers in Ireland had to fight through the culture of the land, which involved a strong liking for drinking.

If you were under eighteen and you wanted to train to be a Pioneer, you were called a Probationer and there were pins for that too. I didn't see the point of that though since you weren't supposed to drink before you were eighteen anyway. It was like being on probation for life until after you became eighteen. In Ireland there was something wrong with you if you didn't drink, unless you were a Pioneer, which made you alright, if just a bit too holy. People who didn't drink and weren't pioneers needed checking up on.

Uncle Sean was born left handed. That was bad. So he became right handed. He may not have liked the method of becoming right handed because it involved adults tying your left hand behind your back and making sure you used your right hand until it was at least as good as your left. I thought that this idea must have come from the bright spark who named the back street out of Pomeroy 'Back Street' and that maybe this bright spark was a doctor. You see, it's all because the Devil is left handed. But Sean developed an affliction. He became ambidextrous. This was an affliction in its own right because no-one knew what the word meant never mind how to spell it. But now he could use both hands. The treatment worked. It still works today. Modern footballers, Gaelic and soccer players, have to learn to kick with both feet. That must be because the Devil couldn't kick football to save his life, with either foot.

Uncle Sean had another odd condition. Most human beings speak as they exhale, drawing breath between sentences. Sean didn't let the breathing in bit interrupt his flow of conversation, literally not wasting a breath. It gave his spoken sentences a curious wheezing lilt, or at least half of them anyway.

My Uncle wasn't around. He was probably out looking after the cows and making sure they spoke Gaelic too and weren't drinking.

"What are they teaching you at school Eamon?"

"The Potato Famine," I replied. "More than a million dead and the population shrunk from eight million to five million."

"That was a tough time," she replied. I checked her out a bit more 'cos she looked like she was actually able to remember it even though it was a hundred and thirty years before. She couldn't remember it but she said that her granny could. This blew my mind.

"Tell me what she said about it?" I asked.

At this point, my cousin Colm came in. He was my age, just-about, with a load of floppy blonde hair and looked like an older version of my bother Brendan. He waved at me, said nothing and sat on the floor beside Brid listening to his mother.

"Well, the folk in the north didn't fare as bad as elsewhere in Ireland. The Protestant farms kept well stocked with food but the ordinary people didn't starve as much as those in the South because they got some food from the Protestants and we had the coastline all around and then there was Lough Neagh which is full of eels."

"Eels!" Colm exclaimed, "Who'd eat eels?"

"You'd be surprised what you would eat if you are hungry enough Colm," she replied. "In Donegal we gathered some types of seaweed that you can cook to keep us going and some that could keep the animals fed." It was the way she spoke about it, as if she was actually there. That had me hooked. It was like time travelling.

"And of course there was lots of fish in the sea and lobsters and crabs and shellfish around the coast, as far as Donegal was concerned. Plus there were always big fishing fleets going out of Burtonport and Killybegs," Aine continued.

I wondered how the people of Pomeroy had fared. The Loughshore, the western edge of Lough Neagh and the largest inland lake in the British Isles, was about eighteen miles east of the village. But there wasn't much in the Lough apart from an abundance of eels. Kieran, Aidan and I had spent a week down there with relatives last year. I remembered the wide expanse of the lough, the flat fields, the evenings that seemed to last forever and the squadrons of midges that would drive you demented if you weren't fast on your feet like I was. Kieran would one day bring eels home from a fishing trip to Lough Neagh and fry them in Mum's big heavy frying pan, cut up into thick chunks and swimming in their own oil, but only he would go anywhere near them to eat.

"My friend thinks Ulster did better because we are smarter than the rest of Ireland," I said.

Aine smiled again.

"Your friend should go to the top of the class."

"The people on that train weren't so smart." This was Colm with a bolt from the blue.

"What train son?" his mum asked.

"The last train to leave Pomeroy station."

The train station in Pomeroy had closed the year before and people were still talking about it as if someone had died. Colm continued, his delivery speeding up like a train. I knew he loved ghost stories, it was getting dark outside so I said nothing and listened. I loved listening to ghost stories too.

"It left Pomeroy on the night of a dark storm – the wind had brought a tree down on the line headin' to Omagh just past the station – the train hit the tree and derailed and crashed in a heap on its side – all 70 people on board were killed – and on Halloween night if you stand on the bridge over the railway down near the station you can hear the screams of 70 dying children." Colm had me goin' until the children bit, as well as the fact that no-one in the village seemed to have remembered the small matter of seventy deaths in the last year or so.

"They were all children?" I asked.

"Yes."

"Where were the parents?"

Colm looked like he'd been rumbled.

"Aunt Aine," I asked. "What's Gaelic for 'total bollox'?" I knew that the phrase I'd heard from Hughie McErlane in Daly's would come in useful soon enough.

Aunty Aine responded in Gaelic words which I didn't understand, but Colm understood and he shuffled off to the hallway trailing wool behind him as he went. That was the last ghost story he would tell for a while.

"Time for me to go Aine," I said, getting up to leave.

Before I went, she told me to stand up straight so that she could measure her emerging geansaí against my upper body. I looked more closely at the half-formed garment. The wool was white and it was in an Aran-knit, straight from the wilds of Donegal The Aran pattern was familiar to me, with big rope like platted strands running vertically through the jumper and triangular motifs zig-zagging up and down against a background of two more simple weaves. How she did that with two little knitting needles was beyond me. It was the only three dimensional jumper in the world. That thing would certainly keep me warm.

"This will be done within the week, I'll drop it down to your mum," she declared. "Oíche mhaith Eamoinn!"

"Oíche mhaith," I responded and headed out the front door and towards the gap in the farmyard wall, clearly defined against the dusk of the southern sky, and then straight down the road for home.

Dad was watching 'The Virginian' on TV when I got in. I had just missed the opening music, my favourite bit, with the cowboy with his black stets on riding his big black horse straight at the camera and the trumpety music going like the clappers.

"How did Pomeroy survive during the famine Dad?" I asked him.

"We just survived, but we were a lot thinner at the end of it," he said.

"Is it true that people started eating grass?" I asked.

"Yes, I've heard stories about that happening, and nettles too. They had it worse down the country than we had it here."

The next morning, I was out kicking a ball at the hedge and then rested a bit, sitting on the grassy bank that was the equivalent of the front garden wall to our house, next to the main road. It was, in effect, a large earth rampart between the road and the front lawn. It was about four feet tall, nearly five feet on the road side. It was wide enough to lie on top of and it was completely covered in grass. It was just about big enough to keep our football in the front garden, just about, and big enough to hide behind if your ball went into the road when a car was passing, the ball to be retrieved when the coast was clear. They don't make front garden walls like that anymore.

On the footpath on the other side of the road I noticed fresh inscriptions on the concrete kerbs. It had been unseasonably warm these past few days and when that happened kids would get wooden lolly-pop sticks and scoop melted tar from the road and inscribe their initials on the kerb stones of the footpath. Publicly defacing the Queen's highway and telling everybody who'd done it, sometimes they would even give you the date of the criminal act as well. The only thing missing was to tell you where they lived. Now and again there would be a little broadcast of an affiliation with Manchester United FC or of an emerging romance at the primary school, GM LOVES SF, with a crudely drawn heart in black tar, a statement born out of jealousy or hope or both, depending on the author.

The earth bank I was lying on was broken only by the entrance gateway into our house. Piers covered in pebbledash with painted precast concrete copings finishing the same height as the bank defined the entrance opening at the road's edge. Then lower walls sweeping inwards and narrowing towards each other on a slight curve ended in two taller piers. These were set a small car's length back from the edge of the road with two metal gates formed in half-inch square steel bars boasting a simple geometric pattern. The gates were brilliant for climbing on and swinging back and forth with strong cast iron hinges built into the piers. The gates were rarely closed, only when there was a funeral procession or a herd of cattle being driven past because the big beasts loved to get onto Mum's front lawn and dance their giant hoof-prints deep into the even turf. Mum would close the blinds and draw the curtains if there was a funeral, as a mark of respect, and we had to stop playing football and ideally disappear altogether as far as Mum was concerned. If we were caught in the open, we were under orders to stand still with our arms straight down by our sides and our heads bowed. Disrespecting a funeral was bad news.

Looking up towards Keeragh I saw the unmistakeable gait of a man I knew coming towards me. I waited until he got a bit closer.

"Still stealing wheelbarrows Al?" I called out.

Joe Toots drove past at that moment in an old Commer van, honking at both of us as he went. He was never out of that van, always on the road ferrying people around to football matches and concerts, gripping the steering wheel as if it was his fate.

I watched Al as he approached me on the footpath on the other side of the road. Al seemed to be always wheeling a wheelbarrow.

"Hop in and I'll give you a lift young fella!"

Al's wheelbarrows were always empty, which is why I thought he was stealing them, but it meant that I could always get a lift. I lay back in the barrow with my feet resting on the front rim and wondered where he stored all his wheelbarrows. Aloyuisis Beggs was the church sacristan, the Parish Priest's handyman. Plus he rang the big bell at the chapel for Mass on Sundays and for funerals and for Holy Hour on a Sunday. He dressed like one of those men in potato famine era drawings, with black jacket and matching waistcoat, black trousers, white cotton shirt and peaked cap. He was small, dark-haired and wiry with tanned leathery skin. He had a quick-step kind of walk that you would recognise a mile off. It was a walk that ran in the family 'cos young Seamy Beggs, a couple of years older than me, walked exactly the same way.

"Where are you off to today Eamon?"

"Me and Joe Hagan are going to Derry."

"That's terrific lad. And what's taking you to Derry?"

"Roamin' Al, just roamin'."

As he wheeled me, I started thinking about how much of the country I would see today on the road to Derry and about the length of the journey, but I knew I was already halfway there.

The wheelbarrow was great but it wasn't any faster than walking. Walking took up too much time and I was a lad in a hurry. That was why I learned to ride a bicycle when I was five, a good few years before any of my brothers. The bicycle wasn't the best bike to learn to ride on though as it was really an adult's bike. It was a big black Phillips 21-inch with a carrier rack over the rear wheel complete with a spring-loaded catch for securing stuff. It was fixed with a dynamo and lights and everything. I loved the sound of the dynamo when you flicked it to the rear wheel although it slowed you down a bit. I thought it was brilliant to be generating your own electricity. With the main support bar on the bike though, my feet couldn't reach the pedals properly so I had to learn by putting my body underneath the bar. I must've looked like a right eejit but at least it wasn't a kid's bike. Later, when I could just about reach the pedals, I had to stand on a bucket or something to get started and stop in spectacular fashion like a cowboy getting off a horse at speed in a John Wayne movie, or simply crash in a heap on your side like the Speedway riders on World of Sport with Dickie Davis on a Saturday morning.

But I wasn't on the bike today.

Al stopped opposite the chapel so I could hop out. He blessed himself as you were supposed to do when you passed the chapel and then held the wheelbarrow steady in a strong grip as I clambered out.

"See you later Al, thanks for the lift!"

Mum had no clue what I was getting up to but she didn't have to worry. I knew what I was doing.

I had arranged the trip to Derry with Joe the day before and I hadn't told anyone. Joe owned one of the shops in the village, just next to the Grotto and drove all over the North picking up supplies. He had one of those Bedford vans with the sliding driver's doors used by breadmen in their white coats delivering food around the country. I loved it 'cos you were sitting high up like a King. Plus there were loads of sweets in Joe's shop and he would always take a good selection on his travels.

"Have you told Ita where we're going?" Joe asked.

"Of course Joe!"

Ita is my mum's name. The Americans would pronounce the 'I' as I when saying Ita but the Irish pronounced it 'eeta'. It is an old Gaelic name. Years later, when my brothers were much older, they would call her by her first name as if she was a sister but it was always Mum that I used.

Once we were on the road, Joe started on his tales and yarns from ancient Ireland. He loved telling me about the fairy-folk, where they lived, their paths and trails, the wild parties they had and how to avoid upsetting them. Now and again he would point out the odd tree, standing alone in the middle of a field. It was a tree where fairies lived. No farmer would cut it down for fear of being cursed for life. Instead they farmed around it.

It took us two hours to reach the city of Derry driving through Omagh and then Strabane on the way. We were very close to the border here, with County Donegal on the other side.

The van passed through one of the gates in the ancient city walls. I expected them to be much bigger but they were in pretty good shape after all these years. Joe told me the story of the Siege of Derry and the Apprentice Boys and King Billy and the Orangemen and all that. This is where it had all started in 1690. This is why the Orangemen marched in Pomeroy around the 12th of July to this very day, celebrating the eventual victory of King William of Orange over the Catholic King James II, at the Battle of the Boyne in 1690. That was 275 years ago but within four years' time the city would be at war with itself for nearly thirty years as The Troubles erupted, like a never-ending echo of those events of centuries past.

I kept my eyes open for Apprentice Boys but couldn't see any little boys in blue suits and them whistling flutes like their lives depended on it as they marched around the place, defending the city with their flutes. I didn't know how you could defend anything with a flute. I loved being in the City though. There were loads of people and cars and buildings far bigger than the biggest in Pomeroy and bridges everywhere and shops on every street. We called into a huge warehouse outside the city walls and Joe stocked his van. It was teatime when we got back to Pomeroy and I trooped in through the back door.

"What have you been up to Eamon?" called Mum, busy peeling spuds at the sink. She was the fastest potato peeler in the world. Even Kitty Connolly wouldn't beat her.

"Just doin' a bit of business with Joe Hagan."

I headed into the living room to find Curly. Curly seemed to be a bit upset with me. He was the same age as me but he had ginger hair and freckles and he wasn't the best lookin' lad in the world. But that didn't matter 'cos he was invisible. He was my imaginary friend. He'd been with me since I was no height. We didn't fight that often except when I was tying my shoe laces – he always tried to mess me up so I couldn't tie them properly and we'd end up fighting. Today though it wasn't shoelaces. I wanted to watch The Monkees. I liked the tall one, Mike Nesbitt, best. It was one of my favourites TV shows but Curly wanted to watch the Pink Panther on the other channel so we started wrestling on the carpet. I got the better of him and grabbed him by the arm and pushed him into the kitchen.

"Mum, me and Curly are fighting. Can you throw him out?"

Mum put down the potato peeler and as quick as a flash leaned over the sink, opened the side casement window, grabbed Curly and threw him out. He landed in a heap in the back garden, but it was on the grass he landed and not the concrete path so he was all right. I headed back to the living room and watched The Monkees. But after a few minutes I began to feel guilty so I wasn't enjoying the show. I walked slowly back into the kitchen. Mum was still peelin' away.

"Mum, can you let Curly in again?"

Mum said nothing but dried her hands on a tea towel and walked to the back door and opened it a foot or so to let him back in. Curly and I headed back into the living room and we watched the Pink Panther.

A little later, I heard a commotion upstairs. I headed up to see what was going on. Mum was standing outside Aidan and Kieran's bedroom door and seemed to be listening to whatever was happening inside. She put her finger to her lips when she saw me approach on the landing.

"They've been fighting and I stopped them," she whispered.

I put my ear to the bedroom door as Mum was doing and it sounded like the fighting twins were now commiserating with each other. I could just make out Aidan saying something to Kieran.

"She gets you so that you can't move your arms and legs and she just beats away at ye!"

Mum and I looked at each other and tried not to laugh out loud.

I went downstairs again to play with my Matchbox cars on the carpet in the front hall. Our carpet was a bit mad. It was so mad it could almost have been church carpet. It had a regular pattern of large cruciform shapes a bit like a Celtic cross with the four ends of the cross turning into decorative finials and going a bit mad in the middle. But it served its purpose. It was better than lino for playing on even though the cars couldn't go flying across the surface as fast as they would on lino, and it was comfortable, especially if you were wearing short trousers.

I would use the space between the mad cruciform shapes as roads and the mad shapes themselves as little villages. The white painted square staircase baluster at the foot of the stair was a gigantic gleaming skyscraper like in New York City and the lino floor of the kitchen was a giant lake, the timber threshold between the carpet and the lino being the beach.

There was a little Virgin Mary statue with a holy water font in it on the pier next to the hall door for blessing yourself as you went out. Protestants thought it was an ashtray hangin' on the wall with water in it to put the cigarette out quicker. On the wall opposite was a framed photograph of President John F.

Kennedy, the first Roman Catholic President of the United States who was Irish really, assassinated two years before. On the wall between the shoe cupboard and the cloakroom was a framed image behind glass of Pope Paul the Sixth with a load of writing on it and a signature which made it even more important. And last but not least was a painted image of the Sacred Heart in the alcove beside the staircase. Jesus was showing he had a heart which was surrounded with a thorny branch and there were rays of light coming out from behind the heart and it was totally real because Jesus' eyes would follow you no matter where you went in the hall. Mum said he could even track you upstairs. So here I was in our front hall, the safest front hall in the whole world, protected by the best US President ever, by the Pope, by the Virgin Mary with extra holy water and by Jesus himself. No wonder I felt happy.

In about ten years' time, the images of Pope Paul VI and JFK would be gone and there'd be a photograph of me on the wall keeping company with Jesus and the Virgin Mary.

After a bit, Kieran and Aidan trooped downstairs looking a bit worse for wear and clearly feeling sorry for themselves. They said nothing as they walked past me and trudged into the cloakroom, closing the door behind them. I had noticed a pencil in Aidan's hand as he went by. After a minute or so, they came out smirking and disappeared out through the front door.

Intrigued, I walked into the cloakroom to see what they'd been up to. The cloakroom was a small room measuring about four feet by eight feet and had simple bare plaster walls, unpainted. The wall opposite the door was stuffed with outdoor coats and boiler suits. On the left was a fuse box and electrical switch gear. The wallpaper in this little room was still a few years off. I didn't need to reach up for the light switch as there was borrowed light from a stained-glass window into the front porch and the porch light was switched on. At first I couldn't see anything out of the ordinary and the lino floor was clear. Then I noticed the distinctive handwriting of a ten year old scrawled on the plaster, about a foot to the right of the black plastic light switch. Here were three simple words inscribed in pencil.

"Shut up Mummy."

There are many different types of leukaemia. There are some types which develop faster called acute leukaemia, which is the type I contracted and others which develop more slowly, called chronic leukaemia. Each type acts differently which is why it is difficult to treat as there is no uniform treatment.

It is hard to tell if you have leukaemia. There are many symptoms but you may not show any signs before you know you have it.

In acute leukaemia, cancer cells multiply quickly. In chronic leukaemia, the disease progresses slowly and early symptoms may be very mild.

Leukaemia is also classified according to the type of cell. Leukaemia involving myeloid cells is called myelogenous leukaemia. Myeloid cells are immature blood cells that would normally become granulocytes or monocytes. Leukaemia involving lymphocytes is called lymphocytic leukaemia.

There are four main types of leukaemia:

Acute Myelogenous Leukaemia (AML) can occur in children and adults and is the most common form of leukaemia.

Acute Lymphoblastic Leukaemia (ALL) occurs mostly in children. This is the one that got me. Its causes are unknown. Some theories link the disease with electromagnetic radiation from power lines. Others connect it with an under-exposure to micro-organisms and parasites in early childhood which effectively fails to fully strengthen the child's immune system. It almost certainly involves a genetic mutation, potentially triggered by a significant illness event such as an infection. Rates of ALL are actually rising marginally in the Western world whilst it is almost non-existent in developing countries.

Chronic Myelogenous Leukaemia (CML) affects mostly adults.
Chronic lymphocytic leukaemia (CLL) is most likely to affect people over the age of 55. It's very rarely seen in children.

Once leukaemia is diagnosed, it will be staged to determine the degree of risk to the patient. Staging helps your doctor determine your prognosis. AML and ALL are staged based on how cancer cells look under the microscope and the type of cell involved. ALL and CLL are staged based on the white blood cell count at the time of diagnosis. The presence of immature white blood cells, or myoblasts, in the blood and bone marrow is also used to stage AML and CML.

Chapter 4
Forest

"Whatever you do, don't cut the bark all around the tree or you'll kill it." This was Kieran's first rule of The Forest.

Kieran and I were halfway up a beech tree on the edge of The Forest overlooking our property.

He had told me the first rule of The Forest before we climbed as if he was some sort of tree-hugging elf lord or something out of Lord of the Rings. It must have been the first and last rule of The Forest 'cos he never told me any more rules. But we never harmed a tree.

He was showing me how to put your initials in the bark with a penknife.

The Beech tree was easier to leave your initials in than most other trees because of the smoothness of the bark. It was also easy to climb as there were branches everywhere. It had by far the best leaves too. They were a lime green colour throughout the spring, darkening in the summer and they were silky smooth to touch and they even had musical properties. You could lick them and put them to your lips and make a sound like a kazoo.

I had climbed to a point where I was level with the roof of our house. I could see the roof of Connolly's garage beyond our chimney and I could see way down our back fields and way out to the wild blue Sperrin Mountains to the North. I could see the tracks me and my friend Adrian had made in the long grass of the field next to Connolly's the day before, where we had carved out a little network of crawling highways. My heart was racing with how high I was. But Kieran was with me, guiding me as I climbed and he was directly behind me now with his hands out like safety barriers on either side of the tree trunk.

He watched me as I chiselled with the tip of the stainless steel penknife into the tree, the fresh sweet smell of the curling green Beech bark strips filling my nostrils as I scribed what I thought were perfect letters. *EK 1966*. Kieran told me to stop sticking my tongue out when I was carving and he guided me down after I had left my mark. I wondered how many centuries my initials would be there for. I wanted to climb more trees and leave more initials.

I was appreciative of Kieran looking after me up there and he must have read my mind.

"Good watchin' takes the head off bad luck," he said. He sounded like a grown-up.

The Forest formed the eastern boundary to our property. Our bedroom window looked out onto it and it helped tell us about the changing seasons and what nature was all about. It was a mix of trees, mostly native, and mostly bent in the direction of the prevailing wind coming in from the northwest. In spring and summer it formed a dense curtain shielding the Parochial House, its outbuildings and the Chapel beyond. In winter, with most of the leaves blown to oblivion, it was a shimmering screen giving glimpses of the holy territory beyond and allowing the crows' nests to form stark silhouettes high up in the tallest trees, unmovable even in the wildest winter winds.

There were steps up into The Forest, concrete blocks laid flat and set into the earth bank, taking you up to a level more than twice as high as I was tall. Two huge Scots Pine trees stood like giant entrance columns a few yards back from the entrance steps, the tallest of all the trees here. But you couldn't climb these as the branches began half way up the tree and the bark was very flaky and sharp so you couldn't shimmy up like Robinson Crusoe looking for coconuts. I thought they were stupid trees. But they had pine cones and these were strewn all around on the ground beneath these giants of The Forest. Sometimes we would pretend that the pine cones were hand grenades which meant we had enough explosives to blow the place to smithereens, there were so many of them.

We basically played soldiers in The Forest. The place was invaded by children on Saturdays and holidays to play these games. We even let girls play as long as they didn't do anything stupid and scream like girls. We'd split up into equal teams and get guns – either toy guns from our house or bits of branches that looked like guns. The girls' guns were always rubbish. They hadn't a clue about guns.

We had rules. You were dead if you got taken by surprise and you killed the enemy by going DE-DE-DE-DE-DE-DE-DE before they did the same to you. This was the sound of a sub-machine gun of course. The girls were rubbish at that too so they mostly ended up dead. If the other team got their machine guns going at the same time as you, then it was a draw and you would start again. One team would stay at the entrance to The Forest and the other team would have a minute to split up and get hidden before we came after them. Sometimes we put a bit of mud on our faces for camouflage.

There was a pathway that wound around The Forest which you could more or less run through without ducking. My older brothers had made the paths through thick brambles and saplings which formed a tunnel around us in spring and summer. Every now and then there was a little passage leading off somewhere or a chamber carved into the undergrowth. There was a bit of a swamp in part of it which you had to be really desperate to cross because you would get your feet wet and maybe lose a shoe or two. We pretended it was quicksand that could swallow you whole.

The place was like a magical kingdom. You knew you'd reached the edge of The Forest when you could see the grounds of the Parochial House beyond. There was a clearing in the middle of The Forest where a giant yew tree commanded the space. It had a great u-shaped bough springing from its huge trunk that three of us could sit on side by side with our feet dangling five feet above the ground.

"This is the kinda tree that Robin Hood made his bows from," said Kieran.

"Where did he get the arrows from?" I asked.

"From a tree with very straight branches and wee pointy bits on the end." This was from Aidan. He was becoming the joker of the family.

"Can you make me a bow?" I demanded.

"We'll get the right branches later," Kieran said. Because he was the first of the twins to pop out of Mum, technically he was the oldest and always thought he should be in charge. That was fine with me. It was cool having older brothers. You were always going to have less bother from older boys or fights at school if you had an older brother and I had two for the price of one, the exact same age.

"We need arrowheads as well," Kieran continued. "Dad has some lead in the garage. We can use that."

We would be playing cowboys and Indians in no time with proper bows and arrows instead of soldiers but we'd have to lay down the sub-machine guns unless we got a Gatling Gun on the go like the US Cavalry used. There were no branches shaped like Gatling Guns though so we'd have to stick to Winchester rifles and Colt revolvers to play the cowboys. I wanted to be an Indian. The bows and arrows were the real thing. I wondered where I could find a makeshift tomahawk and a quiver for my arrows. I'd need some war paint too, and a big feather coming out of the back of my head.

There was a variation of this game using sharp sticks as knives. This involved more close combat and had a tendency to end up in real live fighting, minus the knives. We had the good sense not to play that game again.

About a decade and a half later, my as yet unborn brother Niall and his wee friend Justin would be playing in these same trails when they would find a grey electrical cable snaking through the leaves and branches of the forest floor. Being true detectives, they would follow the wire to see where it led. It led them to a large metal creamery can, the kind that the dairy farmers used to leave by the entrance to their farms for collection by the local dairy lorry. This one was filled with white stuff with the cable buried in the middle of it. They would even stick their heads in to smell what the white stuff was. They had found the command wire to a massive IRA fertiliser bomb awaiting a passing British Army patrol. The nature of the bomb meant that someone was at the other end of the wire waiting to press a button to detonate the explosive targeting a patrol. Army patrols were a regular feature during these times, either up the main road or through the fields behind our home, cutting barbed wire fences as they went.

The young boys would have the presence of mind to tell older brothers and parents and The Forest was evacuated. The police were called and the bomb defused by an army bomb disposal team. That would put The Forest out of action for a few weeks.

Two years later, a real live gunfight broke out in the same location as the bomb position when an army patrol came under automatic fire from two IRA men up in Keeragh. The troopers in the eight-man unit dived for cover behind Ramsey's farmyard wall on one side and desperately clambered up into The Forest on the other and somehow avoided any casualties. After all those years of playing shooting games in The Forest, here were real life professional soldiers diving for their lives to find some cover under the same bushes where we had hidden.

And a year after that a bomb did go off, attached to a telegraph pole on the corner of The Forest on the side-lane entrance to our property, about fifteen feet from where the creamery can bomb had been. The bomb wasn't that big but a small piece of shrapnel was what killed an unfortunate young UDR soldier, piercing his jugular, his body visible from our bedroom window in the streetlight of a late autumn evening, the silhouette of the broken telegraph pole standing sentinel above the sad scene. Luckily for Niall, not being the most studious of the Kilpatrick lads, he wasn't sitting at his homework in the bedroom as he maybe should have been when the bedroom window on that side of the house came in around an empty desk as a result of the explosion.

Later we set up an arrow-head factory in the garage but this turned into a bit of a disaster.

Kieran was supposed to be looking after Brendan who was not even two at the time. When you're looking after babies you need to keep them away from the arrow-head production line.

Kieran was using a hatchet to chop the lead up into triangular arrow-head shaped pieces. Brendan stuck his hand in to grab a piece of lead and the hatchet came down on his fingers. He started screaming like a banshee. I was expecting to see fingers chopped off but Brendan must have strong bones. The tiny hand was bloody and you could see through to the bone. We carried him to the kitchen sink and put his hand under a running cold water tap. That showed us too much as the water washed the away the blood temporarily and we could see even more about why he was screaming. It looked like he would lose some of his fingers. Kieran wrapped his hand up in a tea towel and we waited for Mum to come home. She was back within the hour and took Brendan away. She didn't even shout at us. Brendan's fingers stayed on his hand but he still has hatchet scars on his left hand to this day.

We played other games in The Forest too.

Every now and then there would be a craze for catapults, homemade jobbies with 'Y' shaped branches cut down from suitable trees and with elastic bands and bent over square-cut pieces of linoleum for ammunition that would sting like hell if you got caught with one. Some mad eejits would use steel staples for ammo but that was asking for trouble. We had rules on this and you could only shoot trees with the staples, not people. You could shoot at trees, and the odd passing car, but you needed to be ready to run like the Devil if the driver stopped and chased you. Not that he'd find you the way we knew The Forest and there was no easy way into The Forest from the main road as it was elevated at the road's edge by a four foot wall of rough stone and then the top was completely overgrown.

On Saturdays, we'd be Tarzan swinging through the trees. This was basically because they used to show Johnny Weissmuller black and white Tarzan movies on TV on Saturday mornings so we'd go mad in the trees for a few hours afterwards.

On Saturday afternoons, there was another Tarzan show, a series on the other channel and this one was in colour, which got us out again. Aidan was best at imitating the Tarzan call. I couldn't understand why our Forest hadn't got any big long dangly vines to swing from like Tarzan had in the African jungle. That didn't stop Kieran though. He went a bit too mad swinging through the branches and landed like a sack of spuds after missing a branch. He broke his collar bone and had to go to hospital. But he needn't have worried. An Indian doctor in London told Brendan decades later that if you had to break a bone it was the best bone in the body to break and if you left two bits of collar bone together in a dark room they'd find a way of joining up and healing themselves. I wish we could have told that to Kieran at the time. He was out of action for weeks and was walking around with a sling as if he'd just got back from the war.

The best game in The Forest was played by Brendan and his friend Paul Heatherington about eight years later. I wish I'd thought of it.

They both had quite impressive collections of World War Two plastic soldiers, about two inches high, although there were a few modern era ones floating around too and the odd US Cavalryman without a horse and clearly completely lost in the wrong era.

The battleground was at the entrance to The Forest where there was a reasonably large clearing. Basically you counted equal numbers of your soldiers and prepared to dig in. You hid them behind protruding tree roots or dug trenches in the soft earth and placed them facing the front and the enemy lines, about fifteen feet beyond. It didn't matter if the German Afrika Corps were mixed up with the British Eighth Army for they all faced the same mortal danger. You weren't allowed to use any soldiers that were already lying down or crawling with a gun or anything, they had to be standing up.

Brendan and Paul would count out about twenty stones each, about the size of your fist if you are aged about ten. These were the armaments to be used to bombard the enemy. They took time to carefully construct the defensive lines and then they each took turns to pelt the fortifications with hard aimed throws or stones thrown high up into the air to land like a mortar behind a root defence. It was bloody mayhem and it was bloody brilliant. Whoever had the most soldiers left standing after the bombardment won the game. Some of the soldiers got blown into the bushes and some soldiers sustained injuries from which they never fully recovered. Some got buried in the dirt and couldn't be found. Just like real war I suppose. They'd be finding dead plastic soldiers around that part of The Forest for years afterwards.

One Easter Kieran and Aidan made a hut near the entrance of The Forest using four trees as corner posts. They used bits of wood and shiny corrugated aluminium that they got from God knows where and hammers and nails from Dad's garage. It had a door and everything and it kept out the rain. You could stand up inside and we swept the leaves out the door to tidy it up and nicked a couple of milk crates from Mickey McNally, the milkman across the road, for furniture. It was the best hut ever.

We called Mickey 'The Wee Goose' 'cos he was short of stature and he kind of walked like one. We didn't call him that name to his face though 'cos he had a shotgun and was always shooting at crows and we didn't want him shooting at us. He kept shooting at crows on our roof and damaged the chimney pots. That made Mum mad. What he had against the crows God only knows. Alfred Hitchcock's The Birds had come out in the cinema a few years before. Maybe that was it and Mickey was taking no chances.

But the crows were in The Forest before we were. We were the intruders in their domain, especially when we climbed their trees. Their cawing was a constant background to our growing but you didn't notice it. You only noticed it when they were going mental about something, like a coming storm or a death of somebody important in the crow family. If the Wee Goose actually managed to shoot one of them, then they would all come out of their nests and swoop around their fallen comrade again and again, like some sort of crazy crow wake and you would suddenly think more of the crow than the shooter.

We ate our Easter eggs in our brand new hut after Easter Sunday Mass. We felt snug and secure. Aidan had got carpet off-cuts to make the milk crates more comfortable to sit on. Mickey Connolly from next door appeared at the door and we let him into the hut cause he was only four and had a couple of hard boiled eggs to share and he produced a couple of Cadbury's Fudge bars as well. Lent was over so we were in a celebratory mood and we could eat as much chocolate as we wanted. We had been forced to give up sweets for Lent, at least that's how it felt to me, so we had a lot of catchin' up to do after forty days of sweet-starvation.

We had to be chased out of our hut by Mum to come for Sunday dinner, but we weren't really hungry. A couple of crows squawked out a call in unison that sounded like See You Later as we sprinted down the makeshift steps and left the trees behind, for now.

So that was The Forest. What a place!

A number of tests can be run to assess the progression of leukaemia, including the following:

- Flow cytometry examines the DNA of the cancer cells and determines their growth rate.

- Liver function tests show whether leukaemia cells are affecting or invading the liver.

- Lumbar puncture, performed by inserting a thin needle between the vertebrae of your lower back. This allows your doctor to collect spinal fluid and determine if cancer has spread to the central nervous system.

- Imaging studies, such as X-rays, ultrasounds, and CT scans, help doctors look for any damage to other organs that's caused by the leukaemia.

Of course, none of these were carried out on me.

Chapter 5
Home

Our house was brilliant.

It wasn't massive by any standards but it felt that way. It was perfectly positioned for school, shops, church, graveyard, football field, The Forest and friends. And milk.

Even though we lived directly across the road from the village milkman, we didn't have much cause to use him. This was because Da's brother, my Uncle Sean would deliver a tin pail of milk every morning fresh from his own cows. Unpasteurised and simply chilled, he would leave it on the back step. It was the creamiest milk you've ever tasted. If we were up early enough we would see our uncle, in dung splashed wellies and green farmer's clothes, always smiling with never a bad word in his head. He would always be calling us funny names, like McAtarseny, wherever he got that from. We thought it was make believe but there are actually people living in Northern Ireland with that name. He and my Da were close growing up and remained that way. Sean was a few years older and he was always lookin' out for his younger brother. They were both part-time firemen in Pomeroy's fire brigade and had loads to do with running the Gaelic football club, The Plunketts.

The internal layout of our house was fairly simple but it had loads of places to hide. You needed somewhere to hide when you had as many cousins as we had. Mum had nine or ten brothers and sisters and Dad had about the same so you could get invaded with cousins at any time. We got on with most of them, especially on Mum's side of the family, but you needed to be unfindable if it was your house and you were playing Hide and Seek.

You could hide in the hot press, or airing cupboard as the English call it, or one of the wardrobes in the bedrooms or a clothes' basket in the bathroom, but they weren't the best places. There was a built-in wardrobe in Mum and Dad's bedroom with a little safe built into the wall. That was good. There was the cloakroom tucked behind the entrance porch and if you were little enough you could hide behind an overcoat or a boiler suit if you could hang from a steel coat hook like a monkey for long enough. That was tough though.

There was also the Larder, a walk-in storeroom off the kitchen where we had our big Indesit fridge. As well as the fridge, it was where Mum stored her cooking stuff, her mixer and her mincer, the one you fasten to a table before you start mincing like a proper butcher. The shelves in here were stacked with enough food for years. Mum and Dad got food in bulk from the Cash and Carry in Cookstown because the Kilpatricks owned shops in the village so got the food at trade price. Visiting kids loved the larder. Maybe it was the Penguin bars and the Wagon Wheels they loved. You couldn't keep 'em out of it.

No one else in Ireland had a larder apart from us. It had no windows so you could be completely pitch black with the light off. We'd go in there and strike white stones together to make sparks. I loved the smoky, burny smell that the sparks created, like gunsmoke. Or we'd put a torch behind our hands so you could see the red glow of your own blood. The larder was a bit hard to hide in though because of all the food and the fridge wasn't the best idea for concealment as the Hide and Seek searchers would hear your teeth chattering and you'd turn blue. Then you'd be stuck with some silly nickname – Ice Cube, or something stupid like that.

A pretty good place to hide was the fixed banquette seating in the dining room. You lifted the padded seats and moved the board games to the back and made sure there was a cushion on top of the seat cover when you manoeuvred it back into position with you beneath it to make it look like it hadn't been moved. But that would only work once.

The absolute best place to hide though was the shoe cupboard.

This was a store in the corner of the front hall about a foot and a half wide but deeper than I was tall. It was actually used for shoes in the early days but as time went on Mum would shove photograph albums and board games and that sort of stuff in there. The secret here was that the shelves didn't go the whole depth of the store which meant that if you crawled on the floor of the cupboard to the back wall you could climb up into a hidden secret passage which was a full story in height. The rear end of the shelves formed your ladder. It was the ultimate hiding place. You could have stayed in there for days and no one would ever find you and no adult could reach you as they were too big to crawl in. Even the spiders didn't bother with it. But I didn't use it much as I didn't want anyone else to discover it.

The attic was great to hide in too but it was a bit of a mission to get into when you were only six as there was no loft ladder. The opening was precariously placed partly over the staircase and partly over the landing where Mum had her Singer sewing machine with the cast iron spinning wheel on the side. Basically you had to close up the sewing machine so that the flat wooden lid could form a platform for a chair. You placed the chair on the wooden top of the sewing machine. Then you climbed up the spinning wheel of the Singer onto the wooden top then directly onto the chair. Then you had to move the attic hatch off to one side – it wasn't hinged – and then you had to reach for the edge and pull yourself through the hole. You basically had to be an Olympic athlete to do this and you had to do it all with a torch attached to you somehow as there was no electric or natural light in the attic.

The same dry warm atmosphere in the attic space greeted you each time. It was an aroma of dry cardboard and old leather. The attic was spacious and partially boarded. It had a traditional roof structure, not trusses, so you could walk around and I could stand up in most of it. There was the steady *drip drip drip* of a huge galvanised water tank covered with a loose fitting board. You had to keep your hands away from the insulation between the rafters as it was glass-fibre and would irritate the hell out of your skin for hours.

The space was filled with boxes of discarded stuff – old clothes and toys mainly – stuff Aidan and Kieran were no longer interested in. A few things were placed up here for safety – like the beginnings of Aidan's stamp collection sitting just beside the attic opening. He had taken an old Huntly and Palmer biscuit tin and festooned the lid with various colourful stamps from around the world. It looked class. Quite creative was our Aidan. Inside the tin were a couple of stamp albums. Sadly, the attic wasn't safe enough and many years into the future, a light-fingered tradesman installing loft insulation would make off with the precious collection, which had been added to over the years by the other brothers, except Niall, who didn't give a monkey's about collecting stamps.

I scanned the space with my torch. There were old Thunderbirds outfits and a broken Thunderbirds pistol. There was a Scalextric set. Why the hell wasn't that downstairs? A green vinyl Pan American travel bag filled with old Time magazines lay between the rafters near the opening. The TV aerial was just beyond that. There were boxes of Hornby railway tracks and old transformers and railway carriages and miniature stone bridges and cardboard pretending to be concrete arches for the tracks to cross and railway buildings as well. There was a pair of cream coloured binocular-type things that you looked through and pressed a little lever on the side to rotate a cardboard disc with mini images embedded within it. You needed good natural light to see it properly. The images were slide images of Lourdes so this must have come from my mum's sister Aunty Clare, or 'the wee nun' as we called her. We always got letters from her from Sierra Leone where she was doing missionary stuff but she would make a bee-line for Lourdes whenever she could. I spotted an old Batman comic inside a cardboard box. That was coming back downstairs with me.

But I wouldn't stay up there too long 'cos if Mum found my climbing structure to get into the attic, she'd go mental. I lowered myself down from the attic hatch, toes reaching out to find the seat of the chair. This was the most precarious bit. It was a twenty-foot drop from here to the foot of the stair if you missed the balustrade on the landing and I'd need more than an Indian doctor if that happened. I lifted the chair off the sewing machine, removing all evidence of my attic ascent.

I headed downstairs. Pat McGinn had called in to see Dad and the two of them were sitting chatting in the front room. The sun was making a good effort to get through the white metal venetian blinds of the living room window.

Pat was a short man with dark thinning hair and nearly as wide as he was tall with a big round front. He wore braces to keep his trousers up. I wasn't sure if a belt could do what a belt was supposed to do if he'd had no braces. If he fell over on his belly then he would just bounce back up again.

"Well Caddy," my dad said. He would always call us caddies.

"That cub of yours is getting big." I didn't mind being called a cub as Dad would call us cubs too.

"What's that on your lip Pat? I asked. Pat had what appeared to be an enormous elongated wart sticking straight out just above his upper lip below his left nostril. There were bits of hair around it as he wasn't able to shave properly.

At that moment Mum came in carrying a tray with tea and sandwiches. For some reason she was using the good china.

"I'll get rid of that for you Pat," said Mum and turned on her heel to go back out to find something in the kitchen.

"Have you got the cure for it Ita?" Pat called after her.

"No but I know how to get rid of it!" she shouted from the kitchen.

She returned a few seconds later with a spool of white cotton thread and a pair of scissors. She tied a piece of thread tightly around the base of the wart, used the scissors to cut the dangly ends of thread and told Pat to say a Hail Mary. Pat quickly muttered the prayer and looked up expectantly at Mum. He looked like a right eejit with his hopeful expression and white thread tied around his lip.

"Keep it like that for a few days and it'll disappear." She returned to the kitchen. My baby brother Enda had just been born a few months earlier and he was making a bit of a racket in there.

I had my eyes on the sandwiches.

"You shouldn't eat anything either Pat if you want to get better," I said. "I'll help you with these," as I reached for a ham and mustard white bread sandwich. This was one of my

62

favourites, after bread and butter dipped in sugar which, of course, was number one.

"You've got nahan to learn cub!" said Pat as I started munching on the sandwiches and he started wondering if he should eat or not. I stayed there a while in the filtered afternoon sunlight listening to them talking about football and greyhounds and horses.

I saw Pat down the town a few days later and the wart was gone.

"Tell yer ma she's got the cure for warts. And here's a shilling in case you run short of sandwiches." I thanked Pat and pocketed the shiny coin. I wouldn't be spendin' it on sandwiches.

Mum didn't have the cure for anything but she knew loads of people who had the cure for all kinds of stuff.

There were a few seventh sons of seventh sons knocking around in Ireland at the time and they were attracting huge crowds at big staged events. They could cure absolutely everything but there was nothing wrong with us so we stayed away.

The ones with 'the cure' that Mum knew were ordinary people, mostly women for some reason. They could cure sprained wrists, sore backs, nose-bleeds, eye infections, sore stomachs and athlete's foot. They could even cure ringworm and shingles. Generally they had only one cure each but sometimes some women had two or three cures. These cures could be handed down from generation to generation within the family where they originated.

The cure generally involved a prayer of some sort and sometimes they'd tie bits of wool around whichever bit of you needed fixing. The cure for shingles included a piece of 22-carat gold. Only Catholics had the cure. Protestants couldn't cure anything. You could even get a cure over the phone and you didn't have to be Catholic or anything to get it, you generally just had to believe.

In some instances, people could get the cure for you without you even knowing, whether you wanted the cure or not.

In a few years from now my cousin Peter, who would go on to become the famous Gaelic footballer, would contract ringworm in his scalp when he was about ten or eleven, most likely from a metal gate to a field with cows which had the disease. His mother would take him to hospital but no medication under the National Health Service would cure it. In the end, Mum's doctor, Doctor Meehan, having heard about Peter's ailment, advised that Peter's mum should find someone who had the cure for Ringworm. In desperation, my Aunty Sarah tried this and Peter's condition, an open festering sore on the top of his skull, began to clear up, never to return.

An hour or so after Pat McGinn had left our house that day there was a knock on the front door. I opened it to see a tall man in a dark business suit standing on the front step. Behind him was an estate car parked on our front drive which was totally stuffed with stuff. It was a travelling salesman who had come to sell Dad some equipment or car parts for the Upper Shop and the garage. Salesmen called at the house often if they couldn't find him in the upper shop and Dad would always receive them.

"Is your da in?" he asked. Enda was still squawking in the background.

"Yeah, c'mon in. He's in the living room."

As I took him into the hallway, he stopped and looked in towards the kitchen. Mum had brought the pram inside.

It was the Rolls Royce of prams.

Black cotton canvas with a collapsible hood with white braided trim and white linen lining on the inside where the baby was. It had huge wheels, the biggest at the back with white solid rubber tyres and spring suspension. It even had a brake! But it was a bit odd looking, all black and grand and everything. If you wanted to make a new pram for a brand new baby look like a hearse for some mad reason, this is what you would do. It would be at least 40 years before this sort of thing came back into fashion amongst the fashionably rich in Ireland and England. I'd been in it in my time I suppose but it was far too good for Enda. I knew Kieran was already eying up the undercarriage in contemplating how to construct the best go-kart Pomeroy would ever see – at least until the King of the Hill jamboree four decades into the future. We would call Kieran's contraption a truck rather than a go-kart. It would transform this pram into something useful and it would last for years.

Anyway, back to the noise. You could just see my baby brother inside the pram as the hood was folded down. He was wavin' his tiny arms around in little jerky movements like a demented robot.

"There's a baby in the house," the salesman declared.

For some reason this fella was beginning to irritate me.

"That's my brother Enda. He's got a powerful set of lungs on him," I said.

"Maybe he'll sing a few songs when he's older," said the salesman.

I had an idea. Enda was getting a bit too noisy for my liking.

"He'll be a big noise in Ireland one day," I announced, as my plan was coming into shape.

"I'm sure he'll turn out well," he said.

"Do you want to buy him?"

He looked surprised.

"That depends on how much he costs. How much will you sell the wee baby for?" he asked.

Dad was standing leaning against the door jamb of the living room listening to our conversation with his hands in his pockets, trying to supress a smile.

"Sixpence," I declared.

"Done!" said the salesman. He reached into an inside pocket of his jacket and pulled out a silvery sixpence coin. I accepted it and we shook hands. He went in to talk to Dad and they closed the door.

I stayed put, playing with my toy cars on the carpet. I had a brand new Dinky 007 Aston Martin DB5 from the movie Thunderball, with pop-up armour plated rear window protector, pop-out machine guns in the front lights, rotating number plates front and rear, pop-out tyre mincers from the rear wheels and the ultimate, an ejector seat which actually ejected the baddie! It was the best toy car ever. Even my Dinky Batmobile couldn't compete. I hardly noticed Mum bringing tea in to the businessmen in the front room, as James Bond was just about to make another narrow escape from the jaws of death, just below Pope Paul VI.

It was no time until the door opened again, about half an hour later. The salesman was putting on his jacket preparing to leave.

"Don't forget the baby," I said.

"Ach it's all right," he said, "I don't have anything to carry him in."

"Just hold on a second," I said and turned and sprinted through the kitchen and into the Larder. I emerged with an empty cardboard box which used to have Liga baby food inside it.

"Here you go – he'll fit in that."

The salesman put up the palms of his hands in some sort of sign of resignation and started laughing.

"My car is a bit full. I'll pick him up next time."

I thought he'd lost his marbles, after all, we'd shaken on it. A deal was a deal! He'd bought a baby for sixpence and he wasn't even taking it with him! And there was plenty of room on the front passenger seat 'cos I had checked it out. I wasn't daft. He clearly was though.

My plan thwarted, I wanted the eejit to get outta there. What kind of a businessman was he anyway? I hoped Dad hadn't bought anything from him. Stupid salesman. I looked at him darkly as he left the house. I consoled myself with my newly acquired sixpence which I would store safely in my bank.

Enda had stopped squawking. He must have suspected that he was nearly travelling.

Mum came past and cleared away the cups and plates from the living room. She asked me to go down to the Lower Shop to get some 'messages'. This was what she called a list of groceries or a shopping list.

"A loaf of bread, today's newspaper and tell her no news."

The 'her' she was referring to was my Aunty Rose, one of my Dad's older sisters. She ran the Lower Shop so she worked in the place she was born in and where she grew up with Dad. Big block letters in wood above the shop spelt out 'J KILPATRICK'. This was my other granda, James Kilpatrick who had originally opened the shop. It made me proud that our name was on an important shop in town.

Aunty Rose was friendly to us whenever we went into the shop. A little stooped with curly grey hair and a permanently quizzical expression on her face, she was summoned into the shop from the living area behind by the sound of the bell which rang when the door opened. There was a little window between the counter looking out from the front entrance hall to the house behind so you could look in to the shop and make sure you weren't been cleared out by robbers, I supposed.

Rose was dressed the way old aunties were supposed to dress, in dark stuff with some sort of flowery pattern on it and some sort of beaded necklace around her neck. She always overdid it with the lipstick. I don't think she ever left the shop so God knows what the lipstick was for. I suppose she was the eyes and ears of the village and was always fishing for news. I didn't realise that at the time though. She was just my Aunty. The big shop-front window was in the perfect position to look out over the upper part of The Diamond where most of the action was at, including the red telephone box positioned against the wall between Nugent's and Daly's pubs.

Rose lived with her husband, my Uncle Charlie and her sister, my Aunty Agnes. Agnes wasn't quite right in the head and had a fair degree of physical disability as well but she was well enough to tend the shop now and then and she was as friendly as anything. Rose had two children, one of whom was about my age, Eileen, who one day would take over the running of the enterprise and preserve the Kilpatrick name proudly above the shop window.

"Hello Eamon, what can I get you?" Rose asked.

She spoke from behind a large wooden counter that ran along the length of the shop to your right as you entered. To the left were shelves full of everything from spuds to tins of creamed rice. I would have been able to see over the top of the counter, just about, if it wasn't completely overloaded with newspapers. She seemed to be selling every newspaper in Ireland. I wondered how long the newspapers at the bottom of the pile had been there because you'd need a digger to get to them. But then they'd be so old you'd be reading last year's news.

I repeated what Mum needed from the shopping trip.

"A loaf of bread, today's newspaper and tell her no news."

Rose froze. She had been reaching for a Brandy Ball sweet from a large glass jar on the shelves behind her. Not known for her generosity, I always managed to wangle something out of her. She started moving again but it was like time going backwards as the Brandy Ball went back in the jar and the jar went back on the shelf and the lid was screwed back on, tightly. She handed me the Belfast Telegraph and a loaf of Mother's Pride and said nothing. I handed over some money and she gave me a few pennies in change, in silence. There was nothing proud about me as I walked out the door minus my Brandy Ball.

I decided to nip down to Al Lagan's shop. He had just got in the only ice cream machine in the village and I fancied an ice cream cone topped with delicious whippy ice cream. I decided to make it a 99. The stick of chocolate flake coming out of the ice cream would just top it off. I gave Al a thrupenny bit and made my way back home, demolishing the flake first of all. Main Street had a yellowish glow to it as the sun was beginning to set in the direction I was headed. As I passed Da's garage at the top of Main Street, I spotted a couple of older boys up ahead, lounging on Ramsey's wall just where the buildings of the old town ended and Ramsey's fields began. I didn't like the look of them.

On my right was the partially open front door of a townhouse that fronted directly onto the pavement. I walked in through the front door. Immediately to the left was the living room so I walked in there and sat down on the sofa, licking my ice-cream. There was a middle aged woman in the far corner of the room dusting some shelves with a yellow dusting cloth. No chicken wings for dusters here. I hadn't a clue who she was but she must've been the woman of the house.

"Hello son," she said, "What are you doing in here?"

"There's a couple of older boys just up the road who look like they are up to no good. They'll be wanting to take my ice cream off me and they're not getting it."

The woman walked to the window and craned her neck to see what was going on.

"Make yourself at home and finish your ice-cream," she said, "and keep on this side of the road as you go."

I did as she suggested. A few minutes later, my ice cream finished, I grabbed the loaf and the newspaper and I was on my way. The two boys looked at me suspiciously as I passed them on the pavement opposite.

"Nice day for ice-cream," I called over to them.

They glowered back at me but said nothing.

"How was Rose?" Mum asked when I got back home.

"She looked a bit angry," I said.

"What on earth did you say to her?"

"A loaf of bread, today's newspaper and tell her no news."

My mum froze. I thought she looked odd and needed a nickname. Ice Cube or something stupid.

I went into the living room. 'Man in a Suitcase' was on TV. It was getting late but Dad let me stay up to watch it. I must have fallen asleep and Dad must have carried me up to my bed and baby Enda was still keeping quiet.

Leukaemia is usually treated by a haematologist-oncologist. These are doctors who specialize in blood disorders and cancer. The treatment depends on the type and stage of the cancer. The forms of leukaemia that grow slowly don't always need immediate treatment. If treatment is required, it usually involves one or more of the following:

- Chemotherapy uses drugs to kill leukaemia cells. Depending on the type of leukaemia, you may take either a single drug or a combination of different drugs.
- Radiation therapy uses high-energy radiation to damage leukaemia cells and inhibit their growth. Radiation can be applied to a specific area or to your entire body.
- Stem cell transplantation replaces diseased bone marrow with healthy bone marrow, either your own (autologous transplantation) or from a donor (allologous transplantation). This procedure is also called a bone marrow transplant. Before a stem cell transplant, you receive high doses of chemotherapy or radiation therapy to destroy your diseased bone marrow. Then you receive an infusion of blood-forming stem cells that help to rebuild your bone marrow.
- Biological or immune therapy uses treatments that help your immune system recognize and attack cancer cells.

- Targeted therapy uses medications that take advantage of vulnerabilities in cancer cells.

Some form of treatment is needed sooner or later otherwise the leukaemia will kill you.

Chapter 6
School

Spot was licking some milk drops off the bare wooden floorboards of the classroom.

The milk had just been delivered for the eleven o' clock break. It was still healthy to have milk in schools then. Scientists hadn't banned it yet or made it semi-skimmed or anything. A crow had been pecking at the silver foil top of one of the bottles to get to the creamy stuff at the top of the milk. The crow didn't think it was bad for you either, even though crows had been around for a million years. Some drops of milk had spilled on the dark, untreated floorboards, worn from decades of use and the woodgrain prominent when the two galvanised crates had been carried in. Spot was cleaning up.

"Good boy Spot," said Miss Quinn. Spot was her dog and he never left the classroom when she was there. The person who named the back street behind The Diamond 'Back Street' must have named Spot too. He was a Dalmatian, carrying about ten years.

In winter, the milk crates were placed in front of the fire and Miss Quinn would get one of the boys at the front to turn the crates every ten minutes or so, so that we could all have hot milk at break time. The fire was that hot it could boil the milk in the bottle if you didn't rotate the crate. Some of the boys brought in cocoa powder in a jam-jar and a spoon so we could have hot chocolate stirred straight in the bottle.

Miss Quinn had been teaching Primary One and Primary Two at St Mary's School for as long as anyone could remember. She looked like your favourite granny except better dressed with a smart grey woollen two-piece jacket and skirt. With white hair and light framed glasses, she was what you would expect from a teacher if you didn't know what one looked like. I knew all right as she had taught Kieran and Aidan before me and we knew her even before we went to school. It would be the same for Brendan, Enda and Niall after me. In fact, Mum carried out one of her more outrageous manoeuvres a few years later when it was time for Brendan to go to school for the first time. Mum had told Brendan to go down to visit Miss Quinn and take Enda for company. She knew that Brendan was a bit of a home-bird and that he liked staying put. Brendan did as he was told but as he walked through the school playground up to the old school building he wondered why there were so many children and parents around the place. He hadn't suspected that it was the first day of a new school year, his first school year.

He walked into the classroom with Enda by his side.

"Hello Brendan. Take that desk at the back," said Miss Quinn. "Enda, you can go home." Brendan realised in an instant that he had been tricked but his little four year old brain was already too proud to admit that he had been duped by his mum. The seat he took that day would be the same double desk that I was sitting at now, at the back, nearest the door, ready to be first out at break-time.

I remembered my first days at primary school almost two years before. Miss Quinn had handed out little jotters with about thirty lined pages in them. They were about six inches long by three inches wide with a blue manila cover, front and back, held together by a staple.

Then as now, there were about twenty kids in the classroom. I was sharing the desk with Adrian Nugent who lived in Keeragh. This was the first of the new Council Housing estates up the road from our house before you got to Park View, the second. Adrian was ordinary enough looking apart from the freckles. He had millions of freckles on his face. This made him look a bit different which is why I liked him. We had met before but now we would become friends. It was early September and the summer warmth was still about the place. Adrian and I were flicking through our jotters holding them close to our faces and feeling the draft on our cheeks when Miss Quinn spoke.

"Each page will be for each letter of the alphabet. At the top of each page I want you to write each letter in turn. For those who don't know what an alphabet or a letter is, I've written them out for you."

She was holding a black thin cylindrical stick about two feet in length which she called her pointer and she was now pointing at her handiwork on the blackboard written in white chalk.

"We will go through each letter one at a time and write a selection of words that begin with that letter on each page. Any questions?"

No one put their hand up. I was in a classroom of geniuses. Only I wasn't. Half the boys in the class couldn't spell their own name never mind starting to write words in their jotters. One of the Anderson boys was the first to break cover.

"What letter does the word black begin with Eamon?"

"B," I said. Einstein would have been proud of me.

And so we continued. This was how we began to read and write. I had an advantage in that Mum and Dad had made Kieran and Aidan teach me the basics before I hit school. Some of the boys in the class would have been more at home helping their Dads give a pig an injection down on the farm instead of sitting here dreaming about pig inoculation, which was fair enough, if they could spell inoculation, or pig even.

Three years after me, Brendan would have the same drill. Everything was going fine until the class got to the letter I and the first word was 'I'. Brendan put his hand up.

"Yes Brendan?"

"How can a word have just one letter? It's a letter, not a word."

"No, it is a word Brendan. Some words have just one letter."

Brendan wasn't convinced by this explanation and a few troubled moments later he stuck his hand up again.

"Yes Brendan?"

"One letter can't be a word."

"It is Brendan, believe me."

"It's just a letter."

"Come to the front Brendan and hold out your hand."

This is where Brendan learned that the pointer had more than one use as he felt a short sharp pain across his fingertips and in an instant realised that truly, a word could indeed consist of just one letter. He had no trouble after that.

Almost two years after my classroom's journey of conquest of the English language, we were still using the jotters but the vocabulary had enlarged considerably.

"P-R-O-B-O-S-C-I-S," Miss Quinn spelled it out.

This was a big word. Miss Quinn explained that this was another word for the nose on your face or for an elephant's trunk. We all started laughing and checking out who had the biggest proboscis. Kieran Fullen stood up, put his shoulder to his face and started moving his arm around like he was an elephant. We all cracked up laughing. The reason for our excitement was that we knew that Fossett's Circus was coming to town in a few weeks' time and somebody said they had real elephants. We couldn't wait. Kieran Fullen was saved from sharp words from Miss Quinn by the noise of the class next door moving out for break-time. We fled for the door making elephant noises and doing the pretend trunk thing with our arms as we hit the playground.

The school was one of hundreds of National Schools built all over Ireland by the Government around the end of the 19th century to bring education to the poor and the downtrodden, essentially most of the Irish population.

The architectural layout for the schools was based on a simple pattern, repeated across the country. Generally stone-built, covered in dark slate pitched roofs and coated with a sand-cement render, the buildings would typically consist of two large classrooms, with two entrance halls in the middle. Boys went to the left and girls to the right and ne'er the twain should meet. This forced segregation had begun to break down by the early 1960s. The classrooms were heated by large fireplaces, the chimneys of which arose to form the centre-points of the gables which defined the simple architectural form of the building.

There were steel strips poking out of the ground by each entrance step for removing mud from your shoes. I didn't know why the girls needed one of these. They never played in the mud.

Each classroom in St Mary's was divided by timber and obscure glass screens, with the glazing at the higher level of the screen and no gap between it and the ceiling. They looked like they were moveable but I never saw them moved. They were remarkably good at keeping the sound from travelling between the classes.

The classrooms had vertical timber boarding around the walls to the height of the windowsills. The junior classes were at the rear and the big boys and girls were in the front classrooms. The windows were huge Georgian style sliding sashes but the windowsills were set so high above the floor of the classroom that even the tallest boy couldn't see out. I thought that this was a nasty trick and there was no call for it.

The desks were classic double desks framed in cast iron painted black with seats that were hinged to help you get in if you were too fat and a desk top that lifted as well so you could store your books, if you had any. The tilting bit of the desk was on a slight slope which was pretty cool as it made you more comfortable to do your schoolwork. I loved the smell of old wood when you lifted the tilting desk lid.

The upward slope of the desk ended at the hinges and a flat piece at the front of the desk was grooved twice to hold your pencils. There was a dark porcelain inkwell set within a circular hole in the desk at each end which showed you how old they were. Biros had become all the rage since the Second World War so that was the end of inkwells. I didn't know what all the fuss was about. Fountain pens were cool. Dad had a couple knocking around. You could pretend that they were space rockets. The ink was the rocket fuel and the nib was the bit where you sat and steered the rocket and fired at enemy rockets. They were much cooler than some of the eejit looking rocket ships you saw on TV in Flash Gordon on Saturday mornings, but not as cool as Thunderbirds, especially Thunderbird One. That was the coolest rocket-ship ever.

The surface of my desk was standing the test of time well but there were a number of initials of pupils long past etched into the surface. I looked for my Dad's initials in case he may have sat at the same desk decades before when the inkwells were still in use. His initials were the same as mine and would save me carving my own, which of course needed to be done.

The headmaster of St Mary's was Master Anderson, a little ancient gentleman with white hair and a studious, intelligent appearance. We didn't see much of him in our classroom as he taught the big boys.

The school was set well back from Cavanakeeran Road, nestling literally in the shadow of the chapel on lower ground on the chapel's eastern flank. A five-foot high stone wall formed a tight compound around the school, with the toilet blocks situated at the rear of the compound, largely open to the elements but with the toilet cubicles themselves under cover of little slate roofs.

The walls surrounding the school troubled me. I didn't know what they were for. They were taller than me but built from bits of stone so rough that you could climb them easily. And they were so wide that you could run along the top of them. If these walls had been protecting The Alamo then Davy Crockett and Jim Bowie would never have become famous as the Mexicans would have cut the length of the movie by half and Texas would have stayed Mexican.

The school looked out onto a massive playground between the school and the road. The playground was the forecourt. I say playground. It had no equipment of any kind in it but we didn't notice that we were missing anything and we were never bored. It was big enough to run around like a madman and play football in. At the edges of the space the girls would play hopscotch or mess around with skipping ropes.

A stand of laurel bushes separated the chapel grounds from the school grounds, their big shiny green leaves formed a dense hedge far taller than we were which had few gaps to see through and none to crawl through.

The handball alley, a large blockwork construction covered with smooth grey cement render, was situated just behind the school compound. It was a primary focus for the children of Pomeroy playing handball primarily but also, football, tennis-meets-squash, gunball and all sorts of other games and more besides. It even had a viewing gallery high up at the rear with steps formed in railway sleepers for sitting or standing on and a guard rail that couldn't guard anything. It was a single piece of timber running horizontally across, supported on a few spindly vertical timber posts. There were no intermediate supports. A baby elephant could have fallen through the gaps in the barrier without touching the timber guard rail. Amazingly, no one ever fell off and broke their neck.

Some of the best handballers in Ireland came from Pomeroy and they had learned the game in this old structure. It had no roof so if you were no good at the game you kept looking for balls that got hit out of the alley landing in the nettles around the walls outside, which improved your looking-for-balls skills but not your handball.

The school intake was increasing year by year as the population of the village slowly expanded. It would be a few years yet before temporary classrooms would be needed to deal with the increased intake and almost a decade before a brand new primary school was built and the old building would become obsolete for a time.

The handy thing about the school for me was that you could walk home for lunch, either up Cavanakeeran Road or the shortcut which took you behind the chapel, past my piggy bank in the ditch and up the side of the Parochial House. Mum would always have homemade soup and wheaten bread or soup and spuds. She would always give us dessert too which I thought was a bit posh. Dessert usually consisted of either tapioca or semolina or something else ending in the letter 'a'. It usually came with one or two pear halves from a tin. I wasn't dying about these desserts although the pears were good. The tapioca looked and felt like eating frogspawn and the semolina was baby food pretending to be something else. Now and again we got Ambrosia Creamed Rice. No complaints there. If Mum was out working, it was a bit of a disaster 'cos my da couldn't cook to save his life. The only thing he could make was mashed spuds into which he would mash a soft boiled egg. But Dad didn't bother with the dessert which was a plus point so we'd just grab a Penguin or a Wagon Wheel from the larder and sprint back to school to get a bit of football in before the bell was rung and we were summoned to class.

We'd always come home by the shortcut through The Forest and go back to school by the road. Don't ask me why.

On Friday afternoons, Miss Quinn would teach us about Irish mythology. This was my favourite part of the week and I had a favourite story. This was about the young Setanta becoming CúChulainn. He became the most ferocious and fearsome Celtic warrior ever. He started on his warrior journey by slaying a massive attack dog whilst still a young boy with nothing more than a hurley stick and a sliotar, the hurley ball. He then effectively replaced the dreaded hound by becoming the 'Hound of Culain' which is what his name means in Gaelic. He grew to become the chief warrior of the Red Branch knights, the champion of Ulster and defender of the North. The Tyrone GAA badge with the big red hand came from this time as the Red Branch warriors would dip their hands in the blood of their defeated enemies. The stories of CúChulainn's battles and his brilliant death had me spellbound.

One year, during Brendan and Enda's time at the school, a truly terrifying appearance occurred during school hours. It was an appearance of the non-religious variety. Pomeroy wasn't known for moving statues or voices from on high. The temporary classrooms were in place by then, two of them sitting side by side just outside the old school compound on the edge of the playground.

For a number of days leading up to the appearance, rumours had been flying through the town about a wild billy-goat which had escaped from a local farm.

Some said he belonged to the blind fiddler, John Loughran, but no-one seemed to be sure. John was brilliant at the fiddle but how could he look after a mad billy-goat? One of Tommy Devlin's lads had claimed to have seen the goat and described it as having mad devil-yellow staring eyes and big giant devil's horns. He also described the smell of the goat being powerful enough to lay you flat. Every now and again you would be minding your own business around town somewhere and you would get a waft of wild billy goat smell and you would start quaking in your boots. One afternoon during playtime, someone shouted that they could hear something rustling in the laurel bushes. Brendan and Enda were in the playground at the time and Brendan and Paul Fullen went over to investigate, their hearts in their mouths and them on the balls of their feet, ready to get the hell out of there if the billy-goat was in the bushes.

Next thing the billy-goat somehow appeared right in the middle of the playground behind them.

If you know what happens when you put a drop of Fairy Liquid into the middle of a bowl of greasy water, then you'll know what happened next. The school playground never emptied as quick. Some of the younger children were nearly trampled underfoot in the rush to squeeze into the classroom cabins, the nearest point of refuge. Other kids tried diving into the hedge but they came off second best and had to think again. Once safely inside, everyone squeezed themselves to the windows overlooking the playground, climbing over each other to get a look.

Outside, the mad billy-goat was prancing around in the middle of our playground, like he owned the place.

He was massive. He was walking around like a demented matador. He was exactly as the Devlin lad had described except that he had a big shaggy grey matted coat that looked so rough that even the Devil himself would think twice about putting it on. To our horror there were bits of stuff hanging from his horns and somebody said that they were pieces of human flesh. This didn't make sense to me as no-one had been reported missing in the last few days but maybe he'd been to some other town, Carrickmore hopefully, another village five miles distant. There was no love lost between Pomeroy and Carrickmore. The billy-goat approached the classroom. The kids backed away from the windows and the billy-goat sauntered past, like a great white shark stalking a fishing boat, heading in the direction of the handball alley. The children watched his massive, grisly form amble past in silence.

Master McElhatton, Master Anderson's successor as headmaster, went out to see if the coast was clear. He then came back in and escorted those children who belonged in the old building back to their classrooms. He did this in groups, as if to reduce the risk of fatalities should the billy-goat attack the convoys of children. I wondered if the billy-goat could leap over the wall. Probably. Fortunately, that was the last they saw of the billy-goat that day, although the stench lingered.

Plans were made by the older boys to track the billy-goat down and kill it with sticks and big stones, but they were all too frightened to put the plan into action. The mad billy-goat continued to terrorise the neighbourhood, circumnavigating the village for a day or so after the playground appearance and generally stinking the place out, until he was tracked down by a couple of grown-ups with a shotgun. No mercy was shown 'cos he was as mad as a mad billy-goat. And Brendan was put off goat's cheese for life.

In the mid-1960s, the primary school made use of an overflow teaching space in a corrugated tin shed with a curved roof next to the handball alley. It would have looked space age if it wasn't so decrepit. This building had been built as a parish hall and had a stage and all but now it was being used for the intermediate classes, Primary Three, Primary Four and Primary Five. Kieran and Aidan complained about sitting at their desks with their toes going numb in the winter months as the building was uninsulated. There was no fireplace but instead there were a couple of free-standing, paraffin-fired heaters that were about two and a half feet high. There weren't enough of them and they could barely heat anything. I never got the chance to find out what frostbite was about over there. I supposed that they didn't want the infants to die of exposure and the older kids were too clever to put up with the conditions so it was the seven and eight year old children who suffered.

Thirty years later, the building was still standing, just about, and in intermittent use.

A local entrepreneur and a friend of my brothers, Benny O'Hanlon, was at the start of a colourful and enterprising business journey after opening a car body repair shop in the old tin shed. My youngest brother Niall worked with him for a while, learning the trade whilst still in his teens. One morning in the kitchen space, they noticed mouse prints in the bacon fat in the frying pan. Benny set up a trap to capture the culprit alive and sure enough, the little rodent was there the next morning confined within the little cage. Benny reached in and grabbed it by the tail and then reached with his free hand to a nearby shelf for a small gas-canistered blow-torch. He paced over to the big sliding opening doors of the shed with Niall following. He held the mouse up, it wriggling away from its tail downwards and gave it a blast with the blow torch. He then set the mouse on the ground and let it go. It scampered into the undergrowth.

"What are you doing Ben?" Niall exclaimed.

"That's so he can go off and tell his wee mice friends never to darken the door of this establishment again," he responded.

Master McElhatton, or Wee Kevin as we called him and Miss Campbell taught over there in my time at the school.

Once a month, on a Friday afternoon, Master McElhatton came into our classroom to tell us stories. Here was a teacher who got your attention and his shortness of stature did nothing to dilute the respect that he was shown by the boys and girls of St Mary's. He would end up teaching at the school for 38 years.

Master McElhatton was brilliant at recounting the history and mythology of Ireland and even better at telling ghost stories. He seemed to be able to pick his moment to tell his scary yarns, turning off the classroom lights so you knew there were dark heavy skies outside the window. One which had us quaking in our desks was called 'The Red Cardinal' which was a bit like the Picture of Dorian Gray, only scarier. Another of the Master's tales was called 'The Hitchhiker with the Red Bandana'. The ghost stories he told all seemed to have the word 'red' in their title as they all had a red something-or-other in it and they all had a bloody ending. They would be remembered for generations.

The Red Cardinal was the tale of a lonesome student leaving London, having done not-so-great in his exams at a city university, who visited a run-down country estate for shelter, unknowingly heading for a gruesome encounter. The Master would sit at the edge of his desk at the front of the classroom in the telling of the tale and at an appropriate moment, and unseen by us, the big wooden blackboard duster would inexplicably clatter to the floor to shatter the silence and have us jumping out of our skins, or he would slap the desk powerfully with the palm of his hand to deliver the same effect. The movie *Psycho* had come out six years previously and although we had heard about it, none of us had seen it as it was banned across Ireland and we were too young in any event to watch it. There were no other slasher movies in those days so someone who could tell ghost stories that actually scared you was held in high esteem.

It was a compelling tale to our young minds.

The unfortunate student had taken a bus out of the city, but after 50 miles or so north of London, the bus had broken down on a country road. The student looked around to find that he was the only passenger on the bus. It was dark outside and the road was quiet. The driver told the student that he needed to stay with his bus but he directed the student to follow a country lane, the entrance approach of which was a few hundred yards down the road. The student was told that he would find shelter for the night at the old Bishop's mansion which lay at the end of the lane. The driver handed him a cylindrical battery-powered torch and the student set off.

The lane was much longer than he expected and the battery was beginning to glimmer down and fade as, finally, the big stone flank of the Bishop's House came into view, more of a silhouette against the night sky and dusky trees than an identifiable façade, for there were no lights to illuminate the place and no moonlight.

He found what he thought was the front door, a huge timber boarded thing within a vaulted recessed porch with a big black cast iron knocker that he could barely budge. He prised the heavy knocker off its perch, wresting against its hinge, and after a few dull knocks of iron on iron he could see from below the door that someone was approaching from the interior with a light. The door slowly opened to an accompaniment of screeching, un-oiled hinges that set his nerves on edge. An ancient lady, clad in black and almost bent double with age, was clutching a brass candelabra in her right hand with five flaming candles, wax dripping down to cover old wax clinging to the dull yellow metalwork. She stepped back a pace to make way and he crossed the threshold. A few oil-fired lamps set on side tables along one edge of the hallway gave some feeble illumination to the entrance space. The woman gazed at him with neither interest nor pity. She remained silent.

The student explained his predicament, but he needn't have bothered as the old woman raised her left hand and beckoned him with a bony finger before he had finished his sorry tale. He followed her and she showed him into a big stateroom, again barely illuminated by irregularly placed candles. The old lady motioned him to sit at a big mahogany bureau which was directly in front of a central fireplace and she left the room. There was another bureau, this one leather-topped, off to the left with an empty chair beside it. There were other sideboards and empty bookshelves lining the rest of the gloomy interior, but the space was devoid of any sign of recent use with dust coating all surfaces and cobwebs filling all angles and gaps.

The young student was pleased to see that there was a fire flickering in the grate below a great pewter mantelpiece festooned with candlesticks. The flickering glow of the flames set his mind at rest for a moment.

The old woman returned with a glass of milk and some thick slices of white bread and a few knobs of butter. She had still not uttered a word and her expression remained blank as she turned and left the room, closing the door behind her. He thought he heard a key turning in a lock. The only other sound was the *tick-tock* of a grandfather clock from somewhere unseen and, now and then, the odd crack of burning timber from the fireplace.

As he munched on his supper he noticed that there was a huge ornately framed oil painting dominating the space above the fireplace. It was a portrait of a man, an old but fierce-eyed individual, clad in the red cloak and skull cap of a Cardinal of the Catholic Church. The portrait depicted him sitting at a leather topped bureau and staring out from the canvas. His expression exuded malevolence and the student felt the hairs raise on the back of his neck.

He was transfixed by the painting and had a sudden realization of the difficulty he was experiencing in dragging his eyes from the baleful gaze of the Red Cardinal. With a shudder, he dragged his gaze away and examined the rest of the huge painting and noticed that there was a hole in the top right hand corner where the canvas met the frame. There seemed to be some movement behind the hole and as he stared intently wondering what on earth it was, a rat's head suddenly peaked through the hole. The rat spotted the student and then instantly forced its dark furry body through the hole, landing on the mantelpiece and scattering a big brass candelabra to the stone hearth below with a clanking crash of metal on stone. The rat ran along the front of the mantelpiece before leaping to the floor and scampering off into a dark corner, its hairless tail whisking dust as it went. The student's attention returned to the painting but, to the student's alarm, the painting was now missing the figure of the Red Cardinal. The chair in the painting was empty. The room suddenly pitched in temperature and he could see vapour from his own breath.

As the student gazed at the painting, he became conscious of a hulking form to his left, a form which caused the dread to rise up inside him. Without moving his head, he slowly swivelled his eyes and to his abject horror, he saw the Red Cardinal sitting at the bureau staring intently in his direction. It was the painting come to life, or death, he thought. The bureau in the painting was the same bureau that this diabolical figure was now perched at. Before he could react, The Red Cardinal stood up abruptly and with the speed of an athlete, paced directly towards the student, raising an emaciated hand, outstretching, reaching and grasping for the young lad's throat. The Red Cardinal was upon him in an instant, ice-cold, claw-like fingers closing around his throat…

That's when Master McElhatton kicked the heavy metal wastepaper basket across the classroom with a clatter like a thunder roll and there was pandemonium in the classroom. Some of the boys buried their head's below their desks and others stood straight up, ready for a fight. I sat at my desk, gripping its timber edges and scanned the room for a big scary Red Cardinal. My eyes fell on Martin Murray seated two desks to my left. He was ashen-faced and seriously looked like he was going to faint from fright, or worse, die from it.

Master McElhatton flicked the classroom lights back on, retrieved the waste-paper basket and called for calm. He waited a few moments before continuing.

"Are you feeling alright Mr Murray, you look like you've seen a ghost?"

Martin nodded vigorously if unconvincingly.

"What happened next?" asked Mickey Devlin.

"That's for another day," replied the Master.

There was a muted chorus of 'awwwws' from the boys still standing but most of us were relieved that there was to be an interval in our trauma.

The Master dismissed the class and we were done for the week.

We trundled out of the classroom with less exuberance than usual and we went home by the road, instead of through The Forest, looking over our shoulders and anxiously eying the shadows amongst the ditches and hedgerows as we went, getting into our homes as quick as we could, making sure that the windows were shut and the curtains pulled tight.

The Master was a proper storey-teller and that was by far the best of our school lessons.

A man I would have liked to have met is Don Pinkel.

He is one of the world's pioneers in leukaemia research and an unsung hero in this field of medical treatment. He spent most of his life dedicated to eradication of the devastating children's disease.

He was a very ambitious young doctor when he commenced his mission in life at St Jude's hospital in Memphis, Tennessee when I was just two years old. He recruited the staff he would need to set up the administrative and medical protocols in his coming battle. He forged the relationships with other medics and related professionals and he scrounged for the drugs he needed from the pharmaceutical companies. He plagued the authorities and eventually secured grant funding from various federal agencies. He became the key mover behind the establishment of St Jude's Hospital as a front line medical establishment and in its fledgling years, he kept St. Jude's afloat.

He wasn't interested in keeping children with leukaemia alive for a few months, he wanted to grant them life.

Don Pinkel decided from the outset, to put the conquest of the disease at the heart of his medical enterprise.

Chapter 7
Snow

Our excitement was unbridled. Outside the world was white. It was early on a Saturday morning that Aidan announced the news about an overnight snowfall. There was no sleeping-in that morning. Kieran and I bounded out of bed like startled jack-rabbits to get dressed and rushed downstairs. Mum had porridge cooking on the stove.

"Here – put these socks on over the socks you've got." I didn't know that my older brother Kieran was a renowned polar explorer but I followed his instructions. We were getting ready on the back step, in the enclosed space outside our kitchen door. It was darker than usual in this space as the skylight above was blocked with snow.

"And pull your trousers down over your wellies so the snow doesn't get in." The wellies were at least two sizes too big for me but the extra socks helped fill the gaps.

The step was painted in red masonry paint and it was colder today than it had ever been. Kieran pulled a black woollen balaclava from a pocket and put it over my head and then pulled the hood of my black woollen duffel coat over that. He secured the last of the light brown wooden toggles of the duffel coat tightly around my neck and stepped slightly back to look at me. He pulled my sleeves down and checked that my mittens were on properly.

"Scott of the Antarctic!" he declared. I knew about Scott, the South Pole hero, from school.

"He never made it back," I said.

"He might have if he had taken the Irishman on his team with him on the march to the South Pole – a Kerryman called Tom Crean – he was the strongest man in the expedition." I never knew there was an Irishman involved in this famous trek almost fifty years before.

"Did Tom make it back?"

"He did and he went back to the Antarctic a few years later with another explorer called Shackleton."

"He must've liked penguins," I declared. I wasn't sure about Shackleton so I asked who he was.

"Shackleton was Irish too, and he came back as well. And Tom Crean opened a pub in his home village called The South Pole."

"We need to visit that one day!"

"The pub or the Antarctic?"

I hesitated in answering.

"Let's start with the pub shall we?" Wise words from Kieran.

Now that I knew that the Irish had conquered Antarctica and survived I was ready for action.

Kieran turned and went into the garage and came back a few seconds later carrying a pair of enormous wooden planks.

"What are those?" I asked.

"Old water skis," he replied.

"Where did you get those?"

"Dad got 'em."

He pulled a stump of an old wax candle from another pocket and started rubbing it on the bottom side of the skis.

"This'll make 'em go faster."

He grabbed two wooden broom handles which had lost their brushes.

"Where's Aidan?" I asked.

He's gone up to Connolly's to get a car bonnet."

"A car bonnet? What's he want that for?"

"You'll see in a bit."

He went back into the garage and returned with three empty Ferguson Two Sward plastic fertiliser bags. He folded them up into a tight package.

"Here – grab these."

The back door was a ledged, framed and braced timber door painted blue with a spherical brown porcelain handle. It was the portal to our arctic adventure.

Kieran turned the handle and pulled the door towards him. We took our first steps outside. It was deathly silent. Even the crows were speechless for once – they must have been covered in snow.

"Wooohooooo!" I shouted. My voice sounded different, muffled in the new environment.

No one had been outside yet so there were no footprints in the virgin snow apart from the paw prints of an animal – a dog – that had crossed the back garden earlier.

The snow must have been wind-driven as it had partly coated the west and north-facing facades of our home. I looked up and there were giant icicles hanging from the eaves of the roof of the house twenty feet above me. They looked like giant daggers and some of them were as long as my arm.

"Look Kieran – we need to get some of those!"

"Confucius says don't stand under giant icicles if you don't want to get skewered," said Kieran grabbing my arm to move me out of the path of certain death. He was definitely a polar expert, even if I doubted that Confucius ever talked about giant icicles.

"We'll get some of those from the sheds at the Parochial House later. Let's go."

We headed through the gap in the back hedge and into the winter wilderness beyond.

The scene behind our house was like a Christmas card. Snow covered everything. It sat inches deep on the branches of the trees in The Forest. On the ground, the snow was almost a foot deep and deeper where there were drifts. The Sperrin Mountains to the north were barely visible as the snow covered hills blended with the white-clouded sky. The snow had completely buried the tractor's link box that had been sitting there these past few days, turning into a barely perceptible mound. The steps into The Forest had disappeared. Everything was still. There wasn't even a breeze.

We walked across in the direction of our back fields. Vapour came from our mouths as we breathed out, like we were smoking. My wellies made a satisfying soft crunchy squashy sound as I stepped on fresh snow. I wanted to follow in Kieran's footsteps so that I wouldn't mess up the snow too much but his footsteps were too far apart. A robin red-breast was surveying us from his perch on top of a metal valve of the white Calor Kosangas tank sitting just outside our back hedge. The little bird's chest was the only splash of colour in our field of view.

The robin flew off as Aidan appeared from the other side of the gas tank dragging the bright red bonnet of a Mini behind him. He'd attached a length of baler twine to it to make his task easier, clasped tight and looped around his mitten. The bonnet glided easily over the snow.

"Mission accomplished!" he called over to us.

We owned the two back fields beyond where our house was built. Uncle Sean used them for pasture for his Frisians but they were empty of animals today. In time, three huge timber boarded chicken houses would dominate this back space for several years, interrupting the view of the fields beyond, but today it was an open expanse of whiteness.

We veered right towards the entrance to the first field. I climbed the rusty metal gate as the door wouldn't open in the snow. The gate shuddered and threw off its coating of snow as I stepped up. The flat iron steelwork was dimpled with corrosion, reddish brown flakes and flecks dappling my woollen mittens as I gripped the rails, specks landing silently on the snowy carpet of the ground below.

Kieran and Aidan manhandled the arctic travel equipment over the gate. We walked across on the edge of the field. There was a huge snowdrift next to a thorny yellow whin bush beside the barbed wire fence defining the edge of ownership and the boundary to the field beyond. Aidan launched himself into the snowy mound. He nearly disappeared. He reappeared, sitting up grinning and dusting the snow from the furry edge of his coat hood. The look of pure delight on his broad, happy face was priceless. His freckly smile was infectious. He grabbed a handful of snow and started eating. I did the same.

"Remember, don't eat it if it's yellow," said Kieran. I was convinced he could write the manual for arctic survival.

Our first field sloped gently down to the left towards the fence of Brendan Harte's field, the neighbouring property to the west. About three quarters of the way across, the field descended a lot more sharply in the direction of Harte's field and even more sharply towards the hawthorn hedge defining the edge of our second field. We set the equipment down.

"Fertiliser bags first," Kieran instructed.

We grabbed one each and sat on them.

"Lift the front corners and bring them together and do what I do," he said.

He wiggled his bottom in forward movements to the edge of the slope and slowly started to gain momentum. He quickly gained speed and *swooshed* down the hill, leaving a flattened indentation in the snow behind him and then towards the bottom of the slope, leaning and veering left to avoid crashing into the hawthorns. Aidan and I followed at the same time and crashed into each other on the way down and I went head over heels landing face down with a mouthful of snow. It was brilliant. We grabbed our bags and returned to the summit as quickly as we could, breathless.

All three of us got onto the red bonnet. We sat on the flat metal between the internal support struts. It wouldn't budge initially so Kieran pushed us off with one foot and hunkered down at the back. Aidan was gripping the length of bailer twine. Not that it made any difference. Our vehicle was impossible to steer but it was faster than the fertiliser bags and crashing into the hawthorns was unavoidable so you had to abandon ship before then. It was twice as brilliant as we rolled over and over after piling off our red riding hood, snow flying everywhere and the bonnet embedding itself amongst the hawthorn branches and causing a local snowfall from the hedge with the force of the impact. It took Aidan and Kieran to tug sharply on the rope to release the bonnet from the hawthorns. We dragged it back to the top of the hill. After a few more runs on the bonnet Kieran grabbed the water skis and broom handles.

"We need a bigger field. Grab the bags and follow me," he said. We climbed over the barbed wire fence into the field behind the Parochial House and another fence beyond so we were heading towards the hill behind the graveyard.

I tried to make a snowball as we walked but the snow was too powdery to make a proper one.

"What's the difference between snowmen and snowwomen? Kieran asked. He wasn't normally the joke-teller.

"Dunno," I said

"Snowbags," said Kieran

"That's not the answer – its snowballs," said Aidan.

"What do the balls go into?" Kieran responded, looking as wise as Solomon.

Aidan looked at his twin brother as if he had two heads.

"Can we build an igloo?" I asked.

"We can do anything we want," said Kieran.

"Except tell jokes," said Aidan.

We arrived in the new field. The terrain descended evenly to end in a shuck at the bottom, hopefully frozen or we were going to get wet. The bottom of the field was defined by a scraggy hedge and a few paling posts with loose wire indicating a fence rather than acting as one. Kevin McElhatton, a friend of the twins, appeared from the far corner of the field dragging a rope behind him attached to a small wooden sledge.

Kieran put the skis down and put his feet into the big rubber foot-holders. Aidan handed him the broom handles. He pushed himself off with the broom handles and quickly gained speed, bending his knees and tucking the wooden sticks under his arms so they were sticking out behind. He looked like a professional and managed to stay upright as he *wooshed* down the hill before crashing in a heap at the bottom. There was no way of steering the skis so you just crashed in a heap. Kieran gathered the skis and poles and made his way back to the hilltop. I tried next but the skis were too big for me and I crashed after a few feet so Aidan took over. They took it in turns and worked on their crashing technique. I stuck to the fertiliser bags and had a go on Kevin's sledge.

More kids began to show up dragging all kinds of toboggans behind them. None of them were as good as our red Mini bonnet. Then one of the Beggs boys, Noel, turned up with what looked like the brass-handled tray that his mum's good china would usually sit on. I looked at him quizzically. He nodded at me as he reached the top of the slope and placed the tray on the snow. He took a step back and then launched himself onto the tray, attempting to use it as some sort of body board. It didn't budge and he landed face first in the snow a few feet in front of his reluctant carriage. Kieran showed him how to get the best out of it and it worked, after a fashion but the good china wouldn't be going back on that thing as a brass handle went flying on one of Noel's crashes, disappearing into a little snowy ridge.

Our energy levels depleted, we returned home through The Forest. The snow was a little patchy under the pines, the only evergreens in there. Aidan grabbed some giant icicles from the eaves of one of the outhouses behind the Parochial House. We had icicle sword fights until they broke and then we would get more icicles and have more sword fights. We kept at it until our mittens were too wet and our hands started to hurt with the cold. They would hurt more as they warmed up back in the house. We headed in for lunch.

Mum gave us her delicious homemade chicken soup and some wheaten bread she had baked that morning. Dad was in the front room using sheets of newspaper held over the fireplace opening to get a proper draw to light the fire. He had it going in no time. We gathered around the heat and told him all about our snowy adventures.

"You did what with a Mini bonnet? I hope John Connolly doesn't miss it!"

Aidan was grinning, munching a piece of wheaten bread and blackcurrant jam, purple pasting his upper lip.

We dried our mittens by the fire to get ready for round two. We couldn't wait to get back out. I hoped that the snow would never melt.

It was the best day.

Don Pinkel was influenced by pioneering work which was under way at the time in the United States at the National Cancer Institute.

He was to use what he called the 'full armamentarium'. This was like conducting total war on the disease. He would combine all the drugs known to induce remission and administer them to the patient more or less concurrently, at maximum tolerable dosages, over a sustained period. In addition, he would employ radiation of the cranium and the spine to reach the disease's full extent. Finally, he would continue to administer multi-drug chemotherapy for three years to 'eradicate residual systemic leukaemia'.

It would be a relentless and multi-level regimen and one which was prolonged so that the disease would be permanently destroyed. He called it 'Total Therapy'.

His hypothesis was that there were some leukaemia cells that were sensitive to one drug and other cells that were sensitive to another. But if he used all these drugs at once and hit them along different pathways, he could permanently inhibit the development of resistant cells. This intensive approach of simultaneously using multiple agents had been tried previously, with hugely successful results, in the treatment of tuberculosis. Don Pinkel wanted to try a similar approach to Leukaemia.

He realised that his Total Therapy protocol carried huge risks. Each of these drugs, used alone, could have dangerous, even fatal side effects. In combination, it was uncertain what the outcome would be. He worried that he would be pushing young children to the very brink, but he also knew that they were going to die anyway.

Through the early pilot studies, he and his staff would constantly refine the dosages and improve the methods of delivery. His staff would closely follow their patients, checking their blood weekly, and sometimes daily, to determine how they were tolerating each mixture of medicines.

Don Pinkel recognised that he was quite literally experimenting on children. This troubled him but he saw little alternative and he had become tired of being an undertaker.

In those first years, Don Pinkel would sit down with the parents of every new child admitted to the hospital. He would explain his radical approach to them and he gave them a choice to participate or withdraw.

My mum and dad had no such choice.

Not one parent that Don Pinkel spoke to decline the treatment for their children. Many parents hoped that something could be learned from the treatment of their child even if that child didn't survive, such was the gloomy prognosis of the time.

Chapter 8
Garage

It was like going back in time.

"Lookin' for yer da Eamon? He's in the back."

Dominic McCullough was my Dad's worker. He was situated where he was usually situated, in the entrance passageway of the garage. He always seemed to be in a good mood.

It was a space about nine feet wide with dark fair-faced brickwork walls on either side and dusty, recessed mortar joints.

The musical strains of Bill Haley and the Comets' 'Rock Around the Clock'" were audible from somewhere in the rear but I couldn't see where the radio was. Dominic was lying on his back on the ground, holding an electric inspection lamp with its caged protective grille. Its electric rubber encased chord went snaking off into the darkness of the garage interior. Dominic was positioned partially under an Austin Reilly, the front of which was elevated on two metal ramps. His teeth gleamed white through his oil-stained face. He was always oily and he always wore that woollen bob cap pulled tight down to his ears, like a World War Two British commando. His navy blue boiler suit was also stained with oil. Black leather boots completed the picture. A torque wrench and a sprocket set lay on the oil-stained ground beside him.

I could just about walk down past the side of the vehicle without going sideways. My shoulder glanced against the bottom edge of a huge tin sign screwed to the wall on the side of the passageway in green and white, advertising Castrol GTX engine oil.

The passageway opened up into the garage proper. It was ancient. Charles Dickens would have loved it.

There were two more cars in here, a Hillman Imp and a Ford Anglia. It was the kind of Anglia which had sticky out indicators between the front and rear doors instead of indicator lights, like something you would see in The Flintstones.

Between the two cars was a recessed water tank, sunk into the ground so that the top of the water was more or less flush with the floor. This was where Dad and Dominic put punctured tyres into the water in order to spot the hole in the rubber. It had an oily, timber-boarded lid so you could walk on it when you weren't fixing punctures. The lid was off now and the water was moving slightly, rainbow colours dimly reflecting in the oily film on the surface of the water. A little kid could probably drown in that if they didn't know it was there and fell in.

There were a couple of oily benches on the far wall, stacked with engine bits, and a window which was trying to let some natural light in but had to compete with the dirt and cobwebs trying to keep it out. In fact, there seemed to be a film of oil over everything. The smell of engine oil hung in the air. You could almost taste it on your tongue. Behind the Anglia was a metal frame on wheels for lifting engines out of cars. In the far corner was a stack of oxy-acetylene tanks leaning awkwardly against each other. They looked to me like discarded submarine torpedoes. Here was the radio on a bench to the side of the torpedoes. It was an ancient thing encased in dark wood with a circular dial and a cloth-covered speaker. Bill Haley was singing about rocking 'till broad daylight as if he knew this space needed some of that. There were two welders on a shelf below the radio and two grimy welding masks.

I looked up. The ceiling of the space was festooned with bicycle wheels, literally hundreds of them, suspended vertically row upon row. It looked magical. They were the only things in here that had escaped the oil and what little light there was glinted on a thousand silvery spokes and shiny rims. I didn't know what they were there for as this was a garage for fixing cars, not bikes, but I knew that my Dad was the best bike fixer in the world and everyone else knew it too. He must have fixed them so well that he sent the happy owners off with one wheel on their bike and the other one he kept as a trophy and stuck it to the ceiling of his garage.

"Well, how's the caddie?" My Dad's accent was pure mid-Tyrone, but very mild and devoid of the lilting tones of the farmers out the road. His voice had a very soothing quality and came out of a mouth that naturally wanted to smile rather than scowl. Here was a man that it would take a lot to get angered. He was on the other side of the Anglia fiddling with something on the passenger-side front wheel arch.

"We're on our own da. Mum has gone in to Dungannon to see her sisters. You're on dinner duty. Mashed potatoes and boiled egg I suppose." Dad's skills rested in here, not in the kitchen.

Dad smiled.

"But that's not why I'm here."

"What is it you're after cub?"

"I've come for the job."

"I didn't know I was advertising."

"You need an assistant mechanic. Dominic's not copin'. He doesn't even have time to clean his face."

Dad had that expression where he was trying to suppress a smile. He stood up and leaned against a bench, briefly wiping his hands on the sleeves of his dark blue boiler suit.

"Have you any experience?"

"I'm good at lyin' on my back and lookin' at the bottom of cars. And I can hold an inspection lamp."

Dad's expression escaped into a broad smile.

"What about school?"

"That only takes a bit of the day. I need to make some money."

"What do you need money for?"

"Me and Mum need to buy a car. We can't be taking yours all the time."

"Maybe you could help Jim tidy the shop."

"Aw c'mon now da, that'll take me a century."

It wasn't that Jim's shop was untidy, it was just that he was trying to sell everything that had ever been invented and he was cramming it all into this shop.

"Besides, he wouldn't be the best payer, and I want to get my hands dirty," I added.

Dad was scratching his chin, thinking.

"You'd be better off in the shop than in here. There's a lot of paperwork that needs to be sorted."

"You mean like a secretary? C'mon Dad, you can do better than that."

Now Dad looked perplexed. He suffered from migraines and Mum reckoned it was this place causing them so she was determined to get him out to do something completely different. I turned towards the door to the shop. I could tell he wasn't too keen on the idea of me following in his footsteps into this oily future.

"Take some time to think about it Da, and think about a fair wage."

Dad's expression turned into a smile again.

"I'm sure you'll be tellin' me what a fair wage for a six year old is, so you will," he replied.

I headed out of the garage to look for Uncle Jim.

My Uncle Jim was Da's older brother. I never saw Jim wear anything but a light brown hardware store coat and a peaked cap. He gave the impression of being a successful businessman but he was hopeless at actually sending bills to anybody. Some said that if he was paid what he was owed then he could retire immediately. He never said much and only ever grunted a 'hello' to you no matter how eloquently you greeted him. He had as many children as Dad but I wondered how he ever communicated with them. Dad was a man of few words but he was totally wired on the vocabulary front compared to his brother. Jim was civil enough though and he and Dad got on with their business without argument.

The shop that he ran was connected to the garage by an interior room. The shop opened directly onto Main Street. There were two tall petrol pumps immediately outside the shop front with the entrance protected by a recessed porch to the left of the fuel pumps. The shop itself had a counter running down the length of the interior on the right as you entered which was stacked high with brown paper envelopes containing bills and the like. There was an unopened envelope on top of one of the unopened piles with big black handwritten letters pleading desperately 'PLEASE OPEN THIS JIM'. It looked like it had been there for a while.

On the wall opposite the counter were boxes and boxes of different sized boots and wellies set within timber shelves.

The internal room between the shop and the garage was how you accessed the first floor. It was dimly lit from above and there were shelves in here with tins of Duckhams oil stacked high, the yellow and blue colouring distinctive in the gloom.

Above me was where Uncle Jim stored everything for the shop. The little space was dominated by a staircase in the middle. Only it wasn't a staircase. It was the most dangerous ladder in the world. It was wider than a normal ladder but in the space where a ladder would have three rungs, this eejit ladder had one. It was very hard to climb if you were a grown-up and almost impossible if you were six. That didn't stop me. Gripping the rough sawn verticals of the 'stair', I started climbing, hoisting myself rung by rung and trying to avoid splinters in my hands as I went.

There was a lot more light up here and the smell was of dry cardboard and rubber.

I clambered onto the bare timber floorboards on the first floor and stood up straight. It was like standing in a library. Rows and rows of shelves stood above me, crammed with cardboard boxes full of all sorts of things. Here was a selection of galvanised nails. Over there was a bunch of puncture repair kits for a bicycle and beside that a stack of brand new football boots in coloured cardboard boxes. An entire shelf was devoted to brass washers, nuts, bolts, screws, wing-nuts, hose-clamps and silvery rivets. There were boxes of vice-grips and pliers, garden shears and hand-axes, claw hammers and mallets and a pop-out indicator for a Morris Minor. Compared to the oily chaos below, this was like the reading room at Trinity College Dublin, except there were no seats and no books.

The wooden shelves were just wide enough apart for me to walk down without them touching my shoulders. I started darting around them in my own little game and stopped short suddenly, remembering that the opening in the floor that I had just crawled through had no protective guard rail. That slowed me down. The words health and safety weren't forming in my brain but there was a nagging instinct for human survival and that stair opening just wasn't right. I backed away from it.

Uncle Jim appeared, climbing the ladder like he could do it blindfolded. He grunted a greeting at me. He went to a shelf, rummaged around and returned to the shop below, calling to me as he went.

"Mind yerself comin' down."

At least he knew it was dangerous.

I idled a while in my solitude seeing if I could find something on the shelves that I'd never seen before. Dust particles were swirling in the sunlight where Uncle Jim had been. I scoured the shelves. I passed stop-cocks, brass valves and copper U-bends, football boot studs and bicycle pumps and a box of big blue Ever Ready torch batteries. The shelves against the brick walls were packed with manifolds and gaskets and other metallic engine bits.

After a few minutes I found a pair of brick-red rubber gloves. They had a cream-coloured cotton lining on the inside. They looked class. You would be able to pick up loads of stuff with these and not get electrocuted or anything, and you could make perfect snowballs without your mittens getting all wet. These were going on my list for Santa. Beside them were some bright yellow gloves, Marigold they were called, in plastic packages. I hadn't seen these before either. From the packaging they looked like they were for women doing the dishes. I thought I'd put these on my list too for Mum, to stop her hands looking all wrinkly like Granny Farrell's hands, every time she did the washing up.

And then I found what I was looking for. Something I hadn't seen before. It was a long bit of plastic, curved like a shin bone halved along its length with the marrow taken out but also curved slightly. It was in a long clear plastic bag with a bit of cardboard stapled on the top emblazoned with the name of the manufacturer 'Kelly's Handles'. I wouldn't have had a clue what it was if it hadn't told you its function below the manufacturer's name. WELLINGTON BOOT REMOVER. There was only one of them in the box. I looked closer and it had an address below the bright cardboard cover piece saying that it came from County Sligo, in the west of Ireland. There was similar packaging in the box to the right, containing sets of paint brushes, but this elongated instrument seemed to be Kelly Handles' prize product. *This*, I thought to myself, *is how far we*

*have come in Ireland that we need to make things to help you
get your wellys off. If you needed one of these, then you would
need a hell of a lot more help doing everything else in life. I
would need to speak to Uncle Jim about this. What mad eejit
invented this thing?*

My investigations complete, I returned to the ground floor,
managing to stay alive in the descent back down the makeshift
staircase and avoiding the dreaded splinters.

I made my way into the front shop and stood by the counter
at the back of the space. In about fifty years into the future my
nieces, Dearbhla and Alannah, would be occupying this very
space where I stood now, working behind a different counter,
serving customers of the Silver Chopstick Chinese Takeaway
and this place would be a part of history, welly boot remover
and all.

Uncle Jim was behind the counter stacking the shelves
behind. He hadn't noticed me.

"I think this place needs an assistant Uncle Jim," I declared.

"You'd be safer in the Garage with your Da," Jim replied,
passing the buck.

"You look like you could use a hand with the paperwork," I
said glancing at the mountain of envelopes on the counter and
raising my eyebrows.

"It's a pretty basic filing system but it works," he replied.

"How are the wellington boot removers selling?"

"You'd be in the wrong shop if you were looking for one of
those."

I said nothing.

Al Beggs came in through the front door at that point.

"Hello one and all," he called.

"No wheelbarrows in here Al!" I grinned at him. It was
about the only thing missing from Jim's inventory.

He looked bemused, just as he always did.

"What can I do for you Al?" asked Uncle Jim. Al looked
down at his feet.

"I have a problem with my wellys…."

I left them to it and headed down to Joe Hagan's to buy
some sweets. The job-seeking in The Garage would have to
wait, and maybe Kelly Handles had a future after all, at least
for a time.

By 1968, Don Pinkel and his staff had completed the first four studies of the Total Therapy medical protocol. These trials were beginning to offer a glimmer of hope.

Between 1962 and 1967, just as I was entering and leaving the prime of my life, a total of seven patients had gone through long-term remissions and seemed well on their way to full recoveries. Seven was by no means a definitive number but it suggested that the underlying concept of Don Pinkel's Total Therapy was working.

Almost a year after my passing, in early 1968, he and his staff started afresh with a new group of 35 patients in the next phase of developing the treatment of the disease. This would prove to be the watershed year in the history of leukaemia research.

In this study, greater emphasis was placed on attacking the disease's last areas of resistance, certain drug-resistant leukaemia cells that secreted themselves within the membranes of the central nervous system. Don Pinkel's new protocol would retain certain elements from the first four studies, but he would carefully revise the dosages while adding a few entirely new elements, including the use of methotrexate injected directly into the spinal canal. This was to head off meningeal relapse. The results of the new phase of treatment on multiple patients took many months to trickle in.

When the results could finally be interpreted, they were startling.

Of the thirty-five patients being treated, thirty-two attained remission. After five further months, not one had relapsed. A full three years later, half the patients were still in remission. By 1970, these patients were considered long-term survivors and considered to be effectively cured of the disease.

A fifty per cent cure rate was simply off the scale by all comparable results. Nothing even closely equivalent was happening in Ireland or the United Kingdom at this time.

Chapter 9
Beach

We were on the road to Donegal.

We headed for Donegal at the start of every summer, as soon as the school holidays kicked in.

We were in Dad's big Vauxhall Cresta with me, Kieran and Aidan in the back. Enda was in Mum's tummy still and Brendan was up front with Mum as he was still too small to sit up properly in a car. The car was going more slowly than usual and it was slightly tilted upwards towards the front as Dad had hitched the caravan to the Cresta's tow bar, one he had recently fitted We were beside ourselves with excitement. The only dampener was that we couldn't understand why we weren't allowed to sit inside the caravan instead of the car. That would have been the coolest. But that was forbidden. We didn't know why. It wasn't as if we were sitting in the Cresta's big upholstered bench seat all seat-belted and everything. No, it was a complete free-for-all. I'm not even sure if the Cresta actually had seatbelts.

There was music playing as we set off. Dad had fitted an eight track stereo cassette player and had a little pile of Charley Pride tapes. The story of an old American Indian wooden statue, Kawliga, was playing as we set off. Dad had a Herb Albert tape as well, if you were into trumpets from South America.

We kept a special eye on our home-on wheels through the rear window, to make sure it didn't fall off. We didn't worry too much though. We had complete confidence in our Dad's skill in driving with this big thing on the back. He was best caravan-tower in the world.

Donegal was the best county in Ireland, after Tyrone.

It is right next to Tyrone but we would travel nearly a hundred miles to get to our destination and there would be no change from three hours of journey-time with the caravan in tow. It was a major expedition and we would spend the best part of nine weeks up there, with only Dad darting back and forth between home and the coast of Donegal, to keep business things operating.

Going to Donegal was like time-travelling, backwards. As soon as you crossed the border you noticed it. The air was different and it had affected the roads. The tarmac wasn't as shiny as in Tyrone and the paint on the side of the road was all faded, if it had any road markings at all. Even the cat's eyes in the middle of the road were different, especially at night. The cats looked like they needed glasses 'cos if we were struggling to see them in the dark then they couldn't see us. The money was different too. It had the same value but had harps and things and Gaelic writing on the coins instead of the Queen's head and the notes were called punts instead of pounds and they were bigger than pound notes.

Plus there were no horses in Donegal, only donkeys. I didn't know what the donkeys were for, apart from putting on postcards, because I only ever saw them standing in the middle of fields, munching grass.

You had to go through customs on the border, which I found strange and I worried that they would search us. There was a big checkpoint building that you had to drive through and there were men in uniforms with military style caps. I had a few shiny sixpences with me and I wasn't losing them to no Gardai with big hats, or 'the guards' as Dad called them.

"We are now entering the Free State," said Dad. He always said that when we crossed the border into Eire, or the Republic of Ireland as it was also known. He also called it "the twenty-six counties" which excluded the six counties of Ulster that formed Northern Ireland It was also called Southern Ireland, but that didn't make complete sense as it had a bit which was more northern than the whole lot. That bit was Donegal, snaking up past Tyrone on its western flank.

The brilliant thing about Donegal is its diversity as you crossed the county from border to coast. The first bit of it is exactly like Tyrone (apart from the roads), all green, rolling hills and normal trees. Then you hit more sparse territory. The roads get narrower and you head out into bogland and the trees disappear. Little hillocks of freshly cut turf begin to appear, like little pitched roofs with hips at either end but no building below. These perfectly stacked turf mounds sit beside low terraces of freshly cut drills, lines of black water defining their bottom. There is never a turf-cutter in sight although you can spot the odd turf shovel now and again standing in solitary attention next to a turf drill. In fact, you'd never see anyone in these sparse roads. You could barely spot a farmhouse. The only living things you can see out here is the odd sheep scratching around in the heather or an occasional seagull, blown off course from the distant shore.

It was a magical journey through a wild landscape. The sky was always wild too with clouds meandering past more quickly up here than back in Tyrone.

We would always break our journey at the same spot, in the middle of nowhere, where a side road went off northwards over a bridge in the direction of total wilderness. A burbling little river passed underneath the bridge.

We bolted down to the riverbank where you were out of sight of the road. There was no noise apart from the trickling of water over stones and our feet as we scrambled down to a little grassy clearing near the bridge. The grass was short and there were sheep or rabbit droppings hereabouts and a couple of flattish rocks that you could sit on. Scraggy hawthorn and ash trees clung to the stony river bank, darkening the water with leafy cover. There were strings of mossy lichen covering most of the branches, cotton-like trailers swinging loosely in the breeze. It was like time had forgotten this place.

"Can you drink the water?" I asked.

"Depends what's been peeing upstream," Kieran ventured, a survival expert now.

"Why is the water brown?" I asked.

"Because it's running through bogland and the turf makes it dark."

We flicked stones horizontally into the water but couldn't get them to skip like Dambusters as the water wasn't still enough. We got bigger stones and had a biggest splash competition. Mum got out a flask of oxtail soup and some sandwiches.

I took a penny out of my pocket and hid it under a big stone under the bridge.

"We'll look for it next time," I said. "Now it's a lucky bridge."

"It's your river-bank," said Aidan. "Geddit?"

"Very good Aidan," said Dad.

"What's lucky about it?" asked Kieran

"Lucky it doesn't fall on your head!" Mum was joining in now.

I looked up and satisfied myself that the structure was sound for a few years yet.

"It's lucky only if we keep coming back here to try to find my penny," I said, my voice coming back to me, echoing faintly off the bottom of the stone bridge. We started making whooping noises to make the most of the echo. We finished our snack and Mum cleared all signs of our little picnic before we got back on the road.

Mum started singing.

"Oh Ro the rattling bog, the bog down in the valley-oh!
Oh Ro the rattling bog, the bog down in the valley-oh!
And in that bog…."

This song is interminable, with a verse that added something sitting on top of something else each time, from a bug all the way up to a tree, and it could kill half the journey, it was so long, which is why she sang the song in the first place and got us joining in. There were no iPads or TV screens built into the back of headrests in those days and certainly no Pokémons running around Donegal – it was old fashioned entertainment – singing in the car! Mum had a fine voice and she would always get us to join in whether the song was about some mad bog or about a million green bottles hangin' on a wall somewhere.

A few years later, when Brendan was about four, he was coming home from Donegal and suffering car sickness as usual. Mum and Dad were travelling in tandem with my Aunty Carmel and Uncle Franko and they decided to stop at a roadside hostelry, not far from this bit of Donegal, to break their journey. Mum stayed in the car with Brendan but Carmel brought her out a large brandy and port. This is allegedly good for upset stomachs so Brendan was given a wee taste to cure his illness. And another taste. And probably another. The colour returned to his cheeks. Mum started singing.

"In this very house and this very town there lived an old man and his name was Brown." The cure worked, Brendan picked up the singing duties and didn't stop until they were home two hours later, singing the same verse over and over, somehow managing to avoid getting throttled by his older brothers.

After a bit more of the wild emptiness we began to spy in the distance the beginnings of the mountains, a huge ridge crossing our path and dividing the bogland from the craggy Atlantic coastline and its miles of white sandy beaches beyond.

Mount Errigal gradually came into view.

Now here is a proper mountain. If you had to draw a mountain to describe it to some eejit who'd never seen one, this is what you would draw. Errigal is a big, huge conical shaped thing ending in a point, like a volcano. Mount Fuji and Mount Kilimanjaro might be bigger but they weren't two hours down the road from where you lived. It was so huge, I wondered why I couldn't see it from Pomeroy. The only thing missing from it was a bit of smoke threatening serious action from out of its top. But there was no volcano here.

"On a clear day you can see all the nine counties of Ulster from the top of the mountain, all the way to the Mournes," said Dad.

We knew he had climbed to the summit with his brother Sean a few years before. We thought that this was awesome.

The mountain had big white streaky bits down the slopes of its flanks.

"What are those big streaks down the side?" I asked. Mum responded as quick as a flash.

"That's where you're Dad came down the mountain – on his ass – those are his skidmarks!"

We all burst out laughing. Mum was killing herself. Dad couldn't believe she'd just said ass.

"Can we climb it Dad, please? I shouted excitedly.

"Maybe when you are a bit older cub," my Dad replied.

"Will the skidmarks still be there?" I asked. I could see Dad was smiling in the rear view mirror.

We drove on, skirting the foothills around Errigal, until we were so close to the mountain that we were getting sore necks looking up. Little steams of water were now visible trickling down the slopes of the base, forming furrows in the boggy heather-strewn landscape. Occasional patches of cloud interrupted our view of the mountain top.

All of a sudden a valley opened up in front of us, with a lake in the distance forming the valley floor, sunlight glinting off the surface of the water a few miles off. We were skirting the side of the mountain and the road began to fall away dramatically on our left. Large boulders sat on the edge of the road in random locations with rocky outcrops elsewhere, the path of the road weaving to avoid them. In between was a small metal guard rail defining the road edge.

"This is the Poison Glen," said Mum.

"Why is it poisoned?" I asked.

We never got an answer and we didn't care as had just noticed how close we were to the road's edge. Our hearts were in our mouths as the road dropped away completely in parts and the metal guard barrier looked good for nothing apart from gathering rust.

Dad drove steadily on with the caravan in tow. I watched it warily through the rear window. Our travelling home now represented a dead weight that could drag us down into the poison Glen if Dad didn't drive us carefully through this mountain passage. I edged away from the door on my left as we were so close to the edge of the road.

"Look – what happened to that church?" I shouted. The head of the glen had come into view and away down below us there was a church with no roof and what appeared to be bushes and trees growing out of the church floor. We had been to Donegal before but we must have taken a different road that wasn't poisoned and had roofs on the churches. My imagination was running wild. I pictured gangs of Vikings running around poisoning people and stealing church roofs back to Norway, on their longboats. Mum said nothing to put my feverish imaginings to rest.

"It happened a long time ago," was her cryptic response.

"We'll go down and investigate one day when we're bigger," said Kieran. He couldn't wait to get out of the Poison Glen either.

Gradually we came off the dangerous mountain road, passing the reassuring sign of a church with a roof on it and further on, a giant turf-burning power station on our left, white smoke snaking from its tall slender chimney stack and drifting back down the valley from which we had emerged. Maybe that's what had poisoned the glen I thought. Errigal looked majestic in the distance, thin white clouds forming an irregular halo around its summit.

We were approaching the coast now and had our first glimpses of the wild blue Atlantic Ocean beyond. We strained for a better view.

The scenery was changing once again as the bogland receded. There were a lot more rocks within the landscape and the heathery slopes were giving way to wild grassland and dark sandy tidal inlets surrounded by shallow banks. Little cottages abounded, some of which had thatched roofs. There was more life about the place, the odd cow, more sheep and more people and, of course, donkeys! The first big town we hit was Anagray, about the size of Pomeroy, clinging to the craggy coast. This was very close to where Aunty Aine had been born and raised, without a word of English to her name.

We stopped for supplies. We headed into the sweet shop. They had different sweets in Donegal, another brilliant thing about the place. Fry's Chocolate Cream with green filling, Emerald orange sucking sweets with chocolate in the centre, toffee chocolate eclairs with more chocolate in the centre, Tiffin bars, Silvermints, Club Orange fizzy drink and King crisps. You couldn't get this stuff in Tyrone. They also had Kimberly, Mikado and Coconut Cream biscuits and Jacob's Fig Rolls. You could even eat the Liga baby biscuits even though you weren't a baby. The real food was different too. Galtee Cheese was covered in foil that took you about a day to remove and then you remembered that the cheese was orange. But we loved it.

And then there was the milk. The milk in Donegal didn't come in bottles or creamery cans like back home. It came in pint-sized cardboard packages in the shape of a pyramid that you had to snip the corner off to pour the milk. It was the only bit of Donegal that looked space age. And the milk in these little pyramids tasted different but was just as good as Uncle Sean's milk which we couldn't believe.

"Make sure you snip the right corner off Eamon," Aidan would always say, "… you don't want yer milk draining off into the sand." He was a right joker.

The coolest thing about the milk packages was the containers that they were stored in when you went into the shop. They were basically hexagonal buckets about the size of a normal bucket that you could store hundreds of the things in with no fresh air between them. Einstein must have had a wee holiday in Donegal and decided to invent an efficient bucket to hold these things, because you couldn't carry more than two of the wee slippery pyramids at a time or you needed a bag to put them in.

Suitably stocked, we got into the car for the last leg of our journey, a matter of a few miles.

Outside Anagray, we spotted a sign for Carrickfin. It was one of the black and white road signs that you saw when you crossed the border, with raised black lettering on a white background, bigger words in Gaelic, smaller words in English. Dad spoke.

"Your Uncle Sean says that Carrickfin is the best beach in Ireland. We'll explore it later." He was right. This would become the number one summer destination for the Kilpatrick clan in the years hence and even the construction of an airport in twenty years' time behind its long white sandy shore would not spoil its wild beauty.

We were headed for Mullach Dearg which had more of a Terrible Beauty. Mullach Dearg translates as Red Peak in Gaelic. Within five minutes, we spotted another sign-post and Dad turned off the main road, crossing a cattle grate into what looked like a field. There was the barely legible imprint of a vehicle access-way, defined by tyre tracks, winding its way through small reed-topped hillocks, white sand spilling out where the wind was whipping them. The caravan bobbed and weaved behind us on the uneven terrain and Dad took it slow. Within a few minutes we emerged into a clearing. Up ahead there was a flat piece of land that had short grass sheltered by a high grassy bank behind. It rose to about three times the height of our caravan and there was a sandy path leading up and over the brow of the hill. Dad would move the caravan into the space where the flat earth met the slope with the front window of the caravan looking over the beach. There was no one else around and ours was the only caravan in the whole place.

Down to our left, waves were crashing onto a white sandy beach about a quarter of a mile long. It was dramatic. The sound of the breakers filled my ears.

The beach was facing a defined cove with rocky sides left and right containing the incoming sea. The far side of the bay arose higher than the near side with the remains of what looked like a round tower jutting up and breaking the skyline in the distance. I supposed that it was a round tower, constructed to look out for and give protection from marauding Vikings. The headland on the far side was probably where the red peak name, Mullach Dearg, came from depending on the setting sun for the redness. Behind the beach itself the terrain rose in the form of protective sand dunes with giant grassy reeds poking out all over the place. It looked like the perfect beach. We couldn't wait to get out and get down there.

"Not so fast lads," said Dad, "Listen to me."

We stopped short from piling out of the Cresta.

"Remember what I told you last year. This is the most dangerous beach in Donegal. If you want to swim there is a little protected cove around the corner and over that hill in front of us. Mum will show you. No swimming in the big beach."

"Violent undercurrents," said Kieran as we evacuated the car. Now he was a marine expert. We sprinted down the windy path to the beach leaving Dad and Mum to manoeuvre the caravan into position and make ready our home for the next nine weeks.

"The beach is steep as it goes into the water so it's too dangerous to swim in. You get dragged under and can't get back up for air. People were drowned here a few years ago," Kieran the maritime expert continued.

Now Aidan weighed in with more information.

"There's the wreck of a Spanish galleon sunk out in the bay, shipwrecked here after Francis Drake attacked the King of Spain's armada."

I'd heard about Francis Drake singeing the King of Spain's beard in 1588. The history of England and how it affected Ireland was a strong part of our teaching at school, from Primary One onwards. The armada was undone partly by Drake but mainly by a devastating storm in the English Channel and in the Atlantic Ocean where many of the 130 ships were either blown, or attempted to make their escape. Many of the galleons foundered off the west coast of Ireland. They were heavily laden with supplies and treasure as Spain had intended a full-scale military invasion of England, its sworn enemy. Most of the galleons perished in the seas off Ireland and it was said that the dark haired Irish folk of the West Coast owed their lineage to the Spanish sailors and soldiers who had somehow made it to shore, taken in by the local Irish who were no friends of Francis Drake.

I was keeping my eyes open for Spaniard looking locals.

"Let's look for Spanish doubloons on the beach," said Kieran.

Kieran would one day become an avid wind-surfer and would also go scuba diving off these very shores looking for sunken treasure. And one day, during The Troubles, he would be asked to search for and locate a local lad from Pomeroy who drowned himself in a flooded quarry pit outside the village, where the distraught family wished to avoid the police and the British army becoming involved. I supposed that Kieran was the best young lad in Ireland at deliberating with some authority on stuff he had yet to learn, be the subject matter marine, arctic or general survival.

We started searching for gold coins in the shallow water, the waves racing in and receding quickly on the gently sloping sand. We found a dead starfish, razor shells, bits of sea sponge, leathery like slippery seaweed and fragments of an old lobster pot but no doubloons. Dead jellyfish pockmarked the beach every now and then. We weren't touching those. Aidan had been stung by one whilst swimming the year before.

Stretches of the beach close to the water's edge had permanent rhythmic ridges in the sand, as if the sand had frozen itself to mimic the ripples of the water that would cover it on a daily basis. As we stood on the sand with the waves racing up around our ankles, I wondered what had happened to the

Spanish sailors on that galleon. *Had they made it to shore? Was it in the dark? What could they see? Did any Spaniards survive? And where were the Doubloons?* The waves of water receded as quickly as they arrived and seemed to be trying to take the sand from beneath the soles of my feet without touching the sand around. I looked out into the bay. The sea was a beautiful light green colour with white caps flecking up every now and then, darker green in places where there were rocks or shallows below. It looked fresh and dangerous and vast and beyond the horizon lay the shores of America.

"Let's make a dam!" cried Aidan.

We found a spot between big rocky formations where we knew the incoming water would reach and we planned to literally stem the tide. Kieran sprinted up to get a shovel from the caravan while me and Aidan started marking out the construction lines between the two rocky outcrops about twelve feet apart. Kieran returned and the twins started digging to create a sand bank dam. Kieran told me to smooth the walls of the dam to make it more resistant to the incoming tide as he started on a secondary dam. I set to work with my hands, like a professional plasterer. Within a few minutes, foam edged frontrunners of the tide were lapping at the base of our construction. We got behind the dam. The trench we were digging had filled with groundwater. We kept piling more sand onto the dam. The tide rose. The dam held! The tide kept rising though and within a few minutes a large wave came snaking over the top of the dam and our defence was breached. We retreated behind the second dam and started digging like our lives depended on it to make it higher and stronger. This one held for longer. Mum called us for dinner from above. We didn't want to leave but the sea air had made us ravenous. We left the sea to return the beach to normal dam-less topography.

"We need a bigger shovel," said Kieran as we sprinted up to the caravan.

Mum had everything cosy in the caravan. It was beginning to get dark so the gas mantels had been lit, the dull hiss of the gas barely audible in the yellow light. The caravan was big enough for all of us. We would sleep where we were now having our dinner. The table folded up and with wooden slats and an additional mattress the front of the caravan turned into a giant bed. Mum and Dad would sleep at the rear of the caravan in a separate space. There was no TV and we never even missed it. We didn't even listen to the radio unless there was a big Gaelic football match on a Sunday that Dad wanted to hear. You had to light the fridge at the back to make it cold inside. I thought that was weird – fire to make ice – and you had to foot-pump a metal stud in the floor to get water from the kitchen tap. The toilet was outside in a singular blue tent with a chemical toilet.

After dinner we played Ludo and cards until bedtime. Mum made us Ovaltine.

The next day Dad disappeared back to Tyrone for a few days. The beach was within walking distance of local shops so we wouldn't starve. The three lads went exploring the other beaches around the place leavin' Mum to look after Brendan.

Just over the hill from where the caravan was situated there was the little sheltered cove that Dad had mentioned. It was a small sandy cove lined with thousands of giant round stones, smoothed by the waves. This was a safe place to swim as long as you stayed within the cove. Kieran and Aidan found some bits of driftwood roughly the shape of guns and wanted to play the Lone Ranger but they always argued about who got to be the Lone Ranger and who was to be Tonto. I don't know what they were arguing about 'cos Curly and I had to be the horses. I told Curly that we'd play it properly when Aidan and Kieran weren't around but we nearly had an argument 'cos he said he wanted to be the Lone Ranger. I told him Texas Rangers weren't allowed to have ginger hair. That shut him up. He was probably worrying about how many Indians had ginger hair but I left him with that thought.

We had returned to the caravan from out explorations when Kieran noticed something strange down at our beach. A human form was struggling in the water some distance from the shore. We could make out a flash of white skin against the deep green water about a hundred yards from where the waves were breaking on the beach. We shouted for Mum and she appeared at the door of the caravan.

"Someone's drowning!" Kieran shouted.

Mum raced to the edge of the sandy embankment and looked down.

"There are two of them!" she shouted, "Follow me!"

She ran down to the water's edge with us right behind her. "Stay here. Do not move!"

She waded into the water, her summer dress becoming soaked up to her waste as the water quickly became deeper. We could make out the figure of a man with dark hair, floating on his back, clearly struggling and trying to keep another man afloat. As the water came up to Mum's chest, she stopped and shouted.

"Over here – just a little further!" she called out to them.

We struggled to hear her over the sound of the crashing waves, but she got Dark-hair's attention. He shouted something to his colleague and they made a concerted effort to swim a few strokes in Mum's direction. She reached out her hand and moved a little closer to the men and then they were within reach. They came forward a few more feet towards her, half walking, half doggie paddling. She helped them stand upright and placed herself between the two men who clearly needed her support. The incoming waves were making their movements difficult. They approached the shore.

We stood aside as the bedraggled group finally reached us. Both men were in their twenties and both wore dark blue swimming trunks. They had no other swimming gear. They collapsed on the beach as soon as they cleared the water. Both were breathing heavily. The light haired one looked exhausted. They said nothing for several minutes until their breathing became more normal.

"Let's get you up to the caravan where it's warm," Mum instructed.

"Aidan, Kieran, help them up." The boys did as they were told and helped the men get unsteadily to their feet and led them up the beach.

"Eamon – go ahead and bring two big towels."

I did as I was told and met them as they climbed the sand bank. Within another minute they were sitting in the caravan draped in our towels and Mum was heating the kettle to help aid their recovery.

"Where are your clothes?" Mum asked.

"On the far side of the beach," Dark-hair spoke. He had blue eyes and the beginnings of a beard. Mum dispatched us to get the clothes and we sprinted off like madmen, returning about fifteen minutes later.

The men were relaxed now and speaking a bit more freely, clutching mugs of hot sweet strong tea like their lives depended on it. They looked to be in a state of shock as they explained their ordeal in the sea. They'd had no idea that the beach was dangerous as there were no warning signs. They were swimming normally when an undercurrent pulled the lighter haired one below the surface. Dark-hair swam below to save his friend but they soon became exhausted swimming against a tide which wanted to sweep them out to see. When they saw Mum, Dark-hair was able to summon a final bout of energy and he said that it was that which saved them. They had the same accent as us so I assumed they were from Tyrone.

It was eight years later when Mum was sitting on an Air Lingus airliner flying out of Dublin Airport and bound for New York when the an announcement was made on the airplane's public address system.

"This is the Captain speaking. Could Mrs Ita Kilpatrick please come to the cabin at the front of the plane?"

Mum was travelling alone and didn't hide the look of surprise as she undid her seatbelt and made her way to the front of the plane. A green clad stewardess opened the door and showed mum in. A dark haired man with the start of a beard turned from his Captain's seat to greet Ita.

"I never thanked you properly for saving my life," said Dark-hair.

The rest of the summer was a blast. We went to Burtonport, the fishing village that Aunty Aine had talked about. It was stuffed with trawlers and the overpowering smell of fish. This was one of two fishing ports in Donegal, two of the largest in Ireland. I remembered Aunty Aine talking about the famine. You couldn't starve here if you tried. In the years to come Aunty Carmel would move up here from Tyrone and open a pub called the Aran Bar which would go on to become the Lobster Pot, one of the best pub-restaurants in the district.

Dad took us over to Carrickfin to visit Uncle Sean and his family in his caravan.

Uncle Sean had been right. The place was stunning. It was totally unspoiled by any form of tourism and the only ones who seemed to know about it were the Kilpatricks and a few sheep wandering aimlessly about the place. Unlike Mullach Dearg, the beach was safe for swimming with golden sand and rock formations of all shapes and sizes everywhere. When the tide came in it formed rivers between the rock formations that you could dive into.

The rocks were all one identical colour, light pinky-brown with dark flecks and quartzy material giving a hint of sparkliness. One of the rocks at the top of the beach was in the shape of a motor-bike and another was in the shape of a lorry. Uncle Sean took us to Crab Island and his boys, Declan and Pearce, showed us how to catch crabs with bamboo sticks and nets. Later they showed us how to cook them so I had crab claws for the first time. I kept a claw as a souvenir.

We discovered a little square indentation high up in the rocks next to a steep rocky bank which trapped fresh water draining from the hills above and we named it Saint Ita's well, after Mum.

A few hundred yards behind the beachfront we investigated the Sandy Hills, a giant sand dune with the same white sand as was on the beach, about ten storeys high and longer than a Gaelic football pitch. If it had been any steeper we couldn't have climbed it. When you reached the top, you could see for miles around. Then you threw yourself down the slope rolling over and over.

Aidan found an empty clear plastic bottle at the top that had once contained diluting orange juice. It was one of the super-sized ones with a handle. It was split down the middle and was half filled with sand. He pretended it was a machine gun.

"DE-DE-DE-DE-DE-DE-DE!!!" He sprayed us with automatic fire, the sand spewing out as he riddled us with bullets, like spent cartridges from a real weapon. We dived for cover and rolled down the hill to escape. It was sand dune heaven. We had to be rounded up and physically removed from the place by Mum and Dad at the end of the day.

The only downside of that particular summer was Brendan. He cried practically the whole time. We didn't know why until we got home. The drive home had more crying from him, which Mum did her best to suppress, but as soon as Dad turned the big Vauxhall Cresta into the front drive of our house,

Brendan's eyes lit up, he made some sort of cooing noise like 'aaahhhhaaa' and stopped crying. The twins looked livid and even I wanted to throttle him.

Nine weeks is a long time when you are six and it felt like we had been in Donegal for a lifetime, a wild and eventful one at that. The village looked different after all of that time away. The summer had been hot and the countryside looked parched, as if a filter of amber was colouring my vision, with the grass verges spikey and brown and the paths dusty and dry. I felt uneasy for the first time in my life and didn't know why. Now it was time to get back to normal and deal with whatever was coming.

The emergence of positive results for Leukaemia treatment was a gamechanger.

Don Pinkel's team could barely contain their excitement. They realised that the hospital had made a significant medical breakthrough which was of relevance to the world. Don Pinkel and his team prepared themselves to announce externally that it was becoming possible, for the first time in history, to cure this disease.

Articles were written for the *Journal of the American Medical Association, the New England Journal of Medicine* and other important periodicals.

Incredibly, the evident success of his team was greeted with sharp scepticism from the wider medical Profession.

Many experts and leading clinicians simply refused to accept the historic findings from St Jude's. Some even accused Don Pinkel of being a fraud until they visited St Jude to examine the results for themselves and meet the surviving patients.

Chapter 10
Circus

The posters appeared around the town two weeks before. They were placed in shop windows, plastered to wooden gates and nailed to telegraph poles around the village.

Fossett's Circus, Ireland's National Circus, the poster declared. Big bold yellow letters like you get at the start of a John Wayne western, set against a blue background, describing the venue, Pomeroy, and the date. Two weeks seemed like too long a time to wait. We counted down the days until the date of arrival. Then, on the morning of the first performance the circus equipment began to hit town.

The circus would be pitched on the open ground on Limehill, just beyond the old school building, so within easy reach for me, especially if you took the shortcut through the parochial grounds and around the back of the chapel.

The convoy of vehicles came in from Omagh so I had a perfect view from our big landing window which faced due west. It was the strangest procession I had ever seen. A rag-tag bunch of garishly coloured vans and lorries. There were even a few gypsy wagons but they were being transported by a big lorry. The convoy was mainly made up from Bedford Vans and Bedford flatbed lorries and a procession of horseboxes. Lastly came about ten Volkswagen camper vans, like the one my Uncle Sean owned, but more battered and garishly painted.

I got my wellies on and went to investigate. I sped through the shortcut past the church coming out in front of the school.

The circus convoy turned left at Limehill. The convoy of vehicles formed a line to the left of the open space just to the east of the handball alley and just below the old tin Parish Hall. I could see a couple of Tommy Devlin's lads, Mickey and his wee brother Fay, on the far side of the clearing. Mickey shouted something to me which was lost in the din of the hustle and bustle of the circus workers beavering away between our vantage points. They were perched on a wall of the Salesyard which was just behind their home, as if waiting for the show. Tommy and his wife Jinny were good friends of Mum and Dad so I knew the boys well and their older brother Paul was a good friend of Kieran. Kieran and Paul would be driving articulated trucks all over Europe in the years to come.

I perched myself on the corner of the school wall.

The circus folk had sprung into action immediately, parking certain vehicles in what seemed a pre-ordained plan. Victor Ramsey appeared beside me. He was around my age and was always smiling.

"Move over a wee bit Eamon!" I shuffled sideways for him to climb up onto the wall. Victor was from the farm directly opposite The Forest, so a stone's throw from our house. He was from a Protestant family. You could tell from the names, 'Victor' and 'Ramsey'. You wouldn't find a Catholic with either of those names, not in a month of Sundays, but our families were fairly close and were always helping each other out.

One of the biggest flat-bed lorries positioned itself in the middle of the open space. Two men unfastened canvas restrainers with metal clasps and started unloading long pieces of timber. More men appeared and started laying out the biggest timber pieces in a radial pattern. Victor and I watched from the wall. This was the first piece of work in the setting out of the Big Top. It looked like it would take most of the open space, right up to the rear garden fences of the houses facing Main Street to our right.

I scanned the line of parked vehicles to see if there was any sign of an elephant. There was one particularly large horsebox, maybe the elephant was in that one. A man walked over to the horseboxes. The horses were let out of the boxes and started grazing lazily on rough grass at the edge of the clearing and around the handball alley. There were ten of them, all white, five big ones and five little ones. But there was no sign of an elephant.

Only a matter of minutes had passed but the ring was now being laid, with huge sections of red-painted timber manhandled into place by four men at a time and what looked like a bandstand was being set up at the edge of the ring. The seating was next, bleacher type, in tiers and very quickly put in place. Then came the canvas of the Big Top itself. It came in several bits, strategically placed and connected to the various timber poles and supports. Finally, the hoisting of the tent itself. This was carried out by four teams of men hauling simultaneously on main ropes and smaller guide ropes attached to the biggest of the timber sections. Slowly the canvas was hauled upwards to form the familiar shape. The Devlin boys disappeared from view as the huge blue and white tent went upwards and upwards, almost as tall as the chapel behind me. Other men worked furiously securing posts to the ground, one of them with a huge timber mallet, and others still climbed up little metal spikes in the big posts to place additional cross members which would secure and brace the structure. A group of women came carrying what looked like coal sacks but they were filled with fresh sawdust. The women emptied the material at the centre of the performance area of the Big Top and then spread it all evenly with large wooden rakes.

It was a hive of activity. This routine was clearly well-practised and must have been carried out countless times by this crew over the years all over Ireland.

Victor said he needed to get back to the farm. His father, Reggie, had cows and the farm was always busy. I was impressed. He was only 6 and was already working like a Protestant! I told him I'd see him later at the Circus.

I decided that it was time to go elephant hunting. My field of view was blocked by the stand of lorries and vans laid out in a regular line to my left. There appeared to be some activity behind here, close to the handball alley, so I trudged over to investigate.

Behind the vehicles, the white horses were still idly munching at wild grass close to the side wall of the handball alley. I noticed a few spectators were standing on the gallery of the handball alley but looking at the circus activity instead of watching handball. A few yards further up, a robust looking metal-framed fence had been erected to form an enclosure about the size of six horseboxes. It was covered with canvas sheets tied to the frame and there were big timber stays set at angles on the outside of the frame to support the structure. A gate to the enclosure was slightly open.

As I approached, a circus man came out of the enclosure and fastened the gate securely with a rope latch. He started pacing towards a gap between two large horseboxes in the direction of the Big Top. I could tell he was a circus man because he looked like a pirate. With dark curly hair and brown leathery looking skin, he wore a black leather sleeveless tunic which was worn from use and had a red bandana tied around his neck and a metal ring of some sort around his right forearm. His arms were covered in tattoos and he had two gold studs in each ear. Around his neck was a silver chain with what looked like a huge shark tooth hanging from it. On his feet were what looked like black Beatle Boots which were becoming all the rage amongst adults which you could buy in Willie McKernan's shop on Main Street. On closer inspection they turned out to be black cowboy boots and they looked like they'd seen a bit of action. He was carrying what looked like a large fly-swat but the swatty bit was missing.

"I've come to see the elephant." He noticed me just before he got to the horseboxes.

"You've come to the right place – it's a circus."

"I mean now. Do you know where he is?"

"He is a she," he replied.

"So you do know where the elephant is."

"I'd better bloody well know – I look after her."

His accent was Irish, from way down south somewhere, Kerry maybe, or Cork. He didn't look like a Kerryman though. He must have had Spanish relatives from the Armada days given his swarthy looks.

"Is there just the one elephant?"

"Do you know how many bloody elephants there are on the Emerald Isle? There's more snakes!"

"There aren't any snakes. St Patrick drove them out of Ireland." I said.

"And do you know what he said as he drove them out?"

"No," I replied.

"All right in the back lads?" He pretended he was holding a steering wheel and was looking backwards over his shoulder as he spoke. He started cracking up at his own joke but I was grinning too. That was funny. I'd need to remember that one.

"I can help you look after her – I know a thing or two about elephants."

"Where did a wee lad from Pomeroy learn about elephants?" he asked.

"Tarzan movies," I declared.

He burst out laughing.

"Well, you're out of luck lad. Rani is an Indian elephant and I think you'll find that Tarzan was swinging through the jungles of Africa, not India."

"So she's got smaller ears than if she'd been born in Africa. Besides, an elephant is an elephant. And besides that, Tarzan's been to India in his last movie and met Indian elephants, three hundred of them." The movie Tarzan Goes to India had come out a few years before and had just been shown on TV so I knew what I was talking about.

"You're an expert bejeezus!" His teeth flashed white and gold as he grinned at me. I'd never seen someone with gold teeth before.

"Sam Ashe at your service," he put out a leathery hand, bowing his head as he did so. "Elephant trainer extraordinaire!"

"Eamon Kilpatrick, wee lad from Pomeroy," I said as we shook hands.

"Come with me," he said and turned on his heel and retraced his footsteps back towards the canvas-shrouded enclosure. As he unfastened the rope latch he called out.

"Rani – you have a visitor. You won't have seen one of these before. Here's a wee lad from Pomeroy who's an expert on elephants." He opened the gate and took a few steps inside. He beckoned me to follow.

I stepped into the compound. In the corner stood Rani, lifting huge tufts of hay with her trunk into her mouth and munching away. She was looking at me out of the corner of her eye. She was the biggest animal I'd ever seen. She was head and shoulders over a shire horse and broader than the biggest bull in Pomeroy salesyard.

"Hey Rani, Rani, this is Eamon," said Sam.

"Look at her! She's huge!" I couldn't get over the size of her.

Rani took a few paces and was facing me in an instant, towering above me. I wasn't frightened. Sam was standing beside me and I was a few feet from the open gate. She coiled her trunk upwards like the tentacle of a very large octopus and put the snouty end close to my face.

"Blow into her trunk – to show her that you're friendly," Sam said.

As the end of her trunk came close to my mouth, I gave a gentle blow. Her snout twitched as Rani tried to figure me out. She started sniffing my pocket. I had a brandy ball in there.

She looked amazing.

Wrinkles ripples up and down her trunk. Her big dark eyes peered out of her big grey face and looked like the eyes of a big bloodhound, but even bigger. She had eyelashes too. Just as her trunk met her face two small white tusks came out slightly curving and pointy, about the length of my arm. The rest of her skin was almost as wrinkly as her trunk. She looked like she could grow bigger inside without changing her coat. Her big long legs went straight down, unlike a dog, and widened towards the bottom of her big flat feet. There were four giant elephant toenails at the front of each foot.

"Rani likes you."

"Why do you call her Rani?" I asked.

"It's the Hindi word for queen and she's the queen of the circus."

She turned and headed back to her hay crick flicking her tail as she went and knocked a bluebottle into the middle of next week. She had a bushy fly swat at the end of her tail. We stepped out of the compound and he secured the latch.

"How old is she?" I asked.

"Just a wee bit older than you. She's still growing."

"How did she get here?"

"On a boat from India a few years back, though she wasn't in great shape when she came off the boat in Cork. I helped her get better and I've been training her since then."

"You did a good job."

"I tell you what Eamon. The circus is here for three days and I'll give you a shilling for every day that you keep her hay crick filled with hay and her water trough full. I'll show you where to get the hay and we'll sort out a hose and a pump for the water. And you can hose her down once a day as well."

"You're on!" I couldn't believe my luck. I had an elephant for three days.

Sam showed me where the hay store was and rigged up a hose and a pump connected to a small diesel-fuelled generator that was running constantly.

"A few things Eamon. Always announce your presence before you open the compound. Elephants don't like surprises. Generally stay on this side of the compound near the door. She won't hurt you but she is a big animal and you need to be careful so always stay in eyeshot of her when you are in there with her so she can see you clearly. Oh, and don't bring any of your friends in here or you might spook her. It's just you that's allowed in here."

"I won't." I had my fingers crossed when I said that because Curly simply had to meet Rani.

"And don't be paying for any tickets to get into the show. Tell them you are working for Sam Ashe." He handed me a big tooth like the one that was hanging around his neck. "Just show them this and you won't get any trouble."

"Thanks Sam," I said. This was as good as roaming around the country with Joe Hagan, only twice as good.

"Is this a shark's tooth?"

"It's whatever animal's tooth you want it to be Eamon, but not a mouse obviously. Now don't forget your duties and don't forget the latch. We can't have Rani running around Pomeroy on her own like a mad thing."

"Don't worry, I'll be careful," I said. "There's enough mad things runnin' around the village as it is."

I shoved the big tooth into my pocket beside the brandy ball.

"Where are you from Sam, Cork or somewhere?" I asked.

"Not far off Eamon, it's somewhere alright but I have been wandering all my life. The English always ask me where I'm from and I always tell them the same thing – the west. Then they always ask me, "Is that the north or the south?" and then I look at them as if they're right eejits and you should see their faces." He pulled an eejit-looking face that made me smile. I thought that Sam could tell yarns about his travelling all night.

"Right – I'll see you later lad. I'm also the monkey trainer and there's one of them on the loose." He started whistling The Wild Rover as he disappeared between the horseboxes. I turned back to the compound. I called out Rani's name twice and slowly opened the rope latch. Rani was drinking from the trough, siphoning giant sips at a time into her mouth. She raised her trunk in my direction. I waved. She had enough hay and water so I bid her goodbye for now.

I headed for home. I wasn't sure what to tell Mum and Dad about my new job. *Better if I said nothing,* I thought. On the way back I placed my dinosaur's tooth, for it might as well be a dinosaur's tooth as a shark's tooth, in my earth bank for safekeeping. I would need to find a chain to put it around my neck. I'd give the metal arm bracelet a miss though and I would stick to transfer washable tattoos for now. I was probably a bit small for cowboy boots.

That night was the first performance of the Circus. After dinner, I sprinted back down to see how Rani was doing. It was almost half an hour since I had seen her. I had wolfed down my dinner. Mum asked why I was in such a rush. I told her that Curly had gone missing and I needed to find him and grabbed a banana from the fruit bowl on the way out. I had seen the elephant on the Tarzan TV series eating a banana and thought Rani would like a change of diet from hay. Mum called after me about needing money for the circus but I told her I'd be alright, that I had money in the bank. I remembered to get my dinosaur tooth from my earth bank on the way past.

I called to Rani as I approached the compound. I opened the latch and swung open the gate. Rani was standing there right at the gate as if expecting something. I held the banana out in my hand. She sniffed it and grabbed it by the end of her trunk and moved it into her mouth. She didn't mind about the skin. Elephants could eat twigs and everything. She made a growling noise but it was a happy growl. I heard someone whistling and approaching from behind.

"Good man Eamon," Sam said. "You've definitely made a friend there. I'm taking her now to get ready for the show. Make sure everything is shipshape here and I'll see you in a wee bit." He had his giant fly swat thing in his hand and guided Rani out through the gate and around the vehicles. I checked the compound for water and hay, avoiding the largest lump of poo I'd ever seen. It was cool poo though. It didn't stink much and it wouldn't stick to your shoes like dogs' poo or splash everywhere like cows' poo, or just be a complete disaster like cats' poo but I was glad Sam hadn't asked me to clear that up. I'd need a couple of Al's wheelbarrows to shift it. I made my way to the Big Top.

"Roll up! Roll up! The greatest show on earth is about to begin! Roll up!"

Some eejit on stilts and a stupid looking blue suit and a blue top hat was prancing around at the entrance to the Big Top. He had a big red megaphone in one hand. The ground outside the Big Top was uneven so he was walking like a drunk giant.

"Eamon!" someone hissed to me from below on my left, in the shadow between the bumpers of the two biggest lorries. I looked through the gloom. It was a couple of Kieran's friends from Parkview who had a length of rope between them.

"What's the rope for?" I asked.

"We're goin' to topple the bastard on the stilts with the rope, like a snare, trip him up."

This concerned me. I worked for the circus now and this was bad for business.

"Forget that lads, come with me and I'll get you in for free."

They looked at me quizzically, but dropped the rope. I kicked it under one of the lorries.

They were a head above me in height but followed me to the entrance of the tent. Another eejit in a redcoat with gold buttons and yellow braiding was collecting money. People were beginning to arrive in numbers.

"What do you boys want?"

"We're helping the circus." I produced my dinosaur's tooth.

"One tooth, one entrant," he declared.

"Sorry lads, I did my best." I said to the big boys. They hunched their shoulders and turned and shuffled off into the darkness. I walked into the circus tent and grabbed a seat near the front.

That night I saw a troupe of jugglers, fire-eaters, a lion tamer with two lions, a couple of monkeys dressed in waistcoats and hats not doing a great deal apart from being monkeys, a couple of clowns that the children laughed their heads off at but I couldn't really see what was funny, an amazing trapeze artist girl who was only a bit bigger than me but looked about Kieran's age or maybe a bit more and another eejit spinning plates and juggling skittles who came back later to throw knives.

But the star of the show was Rani.

She didn't actually do a big pile, but she was the most graceful creature in the show, human or animal alike. She lifted stuff with her trunk, stood up on her hind legs for ages and walked around a bit, and playfully knocked Sam over a few times when they were playing football with a giant beachball. Everyone loved it. I saw Mum and Dad and Kieran and Aidan at the end of the show, I'd forgotten they were coming, but I disappeared before Mum could grab me to make sure Rani was home safe.

Sam was in the compound when I entered.

"Well Eamon of Pomeroy, what did you make of the show?"

"She was the best!" I walked over to the giant creature and stood beside Sam. Rani nudged her truck into my tummy, very gently, and continued eating some hay.

"I'll finish off here lad – its time you headed for home."

"Goodnight Sam, goodnight Rani." I waved them goodbye and headed for home.

"Did you find Curly?" asked Mum when I got home.

"Yeah, he was plannin' to run away to the Circus but I talked him out of it."

I headed upstairs for bed. It had been a long day.

By 1973, the results of Don Pinkel's experimental treatment had generally become accepted.

He had found a way to treat my condition, **Acute Lymphocytic Leukaemia** in the central nervous system and the hospital had become the centre of attention in the medical world. Other American hospitals began using Don Pinkel's methodology and were achieving the same extraordinary results.

He travelled internationally only to discover that very few countries had the medical expertise and medical staff to operate the way his team had been able to operate. The Europeans needed time to catch up.

One of Don Pinkel's greatest regrets was that his innovative, ground-breaking protocol exposed children to radiation and noxious chemicals that were bound to cause lifelong medical complications, including other forms of cancer. In subsequent studies, Pinkel sought to reduce the most toxic dosages to minimise this long-term risk. In time, paediatric cancer researchers would dispense with the use of radiation altogether.

Don Pinkel had a fervent hope that science would one day find a vaccine that would prevent the type of Leukaemia that he was attempting to eradicate, removing the need for toxic treatments for patients. His staff worked on a vaccine on the premise that **Acute Lymphocytic Leukaemia** may be caused by a virus and then the disease could be treated in the same way as diphtheria, mumps, polio and measles. This dream remained out of reach to his medical team.

However, Don Pinkel's dream of treating Leukaemia as if it is a virus is now becoming a reality with pioneering research by global pharmaceutical conglomerates. This emerging therapy is called immuno-oncology (IO) and it works by equipping your body's immune system with the tools to kill cancer cells. Your body is helped by the treatment to ward off the disease in the first instance and to develop a long-term memory for killing off tumours thereafter. This is potentially the biggest breakthrough in battling Leukaemia and other cancers since the medical breakthrough initiated by Don Pinkel's team.

Despite the blockage in finding the ultimate cure, the 50 percent survival rate established by Don Pinkel's team held fast and then steadily improved. Today, the key components of **Acute Lymphocytic Leukaemia** treatment remain just as Don Pinkel designed them. Doctors today use many of the same drugs to combat the disease, including vincristine, methotrexate and mercaptopurine that were combined into treatment protocols 50 years ago by Pinkel's team.

The subsequent leaps in survival rates approaching 90 percent were made possible, in part, by the development of better antibiotics and antifungal treatments for fighting infections. The survival rate was also boosted by the arrival of better diagnostic tests for detecting residual leukaemia cells and by the use of genomics to select the optimal drugs and doses for individual patients.

These new techniques and medications have been added to the treatment regime to defeat leukaemia in children, but they have not replaced the basic protocol that Don Pinkel established all those years ago. Today, Don Pinkel's experimental approach is viewed as one of the great triumphs in the war on cancer and is still rated as one of the few successes in halting one of mankind's greatest killers as the search for a general cancer cure continues.

Chapter 11
Hospital

It was shortly after the circus left town that I began to feel a bit strange.

The circus had lit up the town for a few days and I had made a bond with an amazing animal.

I faithfully attended the tasks that Sam had set me for the last two days, with me and Rani getting on like a house on fire. She even lifted me onto her back with her trunk under Sam's guidance. It was brilliant. I felt like I was on top of the world. The bit Rani liked best was getting hosed down with water. She loved it. She would lift her trunk up so I could squirt water directly into her mouth. I would put the last few feet of the hose up to my nose and pretend I was an elephant too. I didn't tell any of my friends that I had a pet elephant because I knew I wouldn't be able to keep them away and they'd torment her to blazes. Apart from Curly. I had to let Curly see her. But Rani couldn't see Curly. Only Mum could see Curly.

I attended all three performances to see my new friend in action, and she never let the side down.

The hardest night was the last night as I would have to say goodbye to my elephant. It was school the next day and I would miss the circus leaving town. I went to the compound for the last time at the end of the show. Sam was giving Rani a hose down.

"I'm doin' yer job for ye Eamon, but it's alright lad, I can see how sad you are." Sam put the hose down and handed me a small bunch of grapes.

"Give her those lad and say your goodbyes."

I held out the grapes to Rani and she snuffled and grabbed them with her snout and put them into her mouth and she let out a low grumbly growl of satisfaction.

"I haven't heard her bellow like elephants are supposed to," I said.

"She only does that when she's really excited or she has something to say. She probably needs a bit of exercise so I'm thinking that we'll let her run out of the town down that big hill of yours before putting her in her box at the bottom of the hill, past the policemen's house. She'll love that. Will you be around?"

"Nah, I've got school."

I stepped closer to Rani and gave her trunk a big hug. She made another of her grumbly growls and I knew she was saying goodbye too. I pulled a banana skin from my pocket and gave it to Rani. It was my parting gift. Sam smiled.

"Next time I'm in this part of the world I'll give you a shout." He pulled out a little brown pigskin purse, fished out three shillings and handed them to me.

"There's your earnings lad."

"Thanks Sam." I pocketed the silver coins. "It's been great knowing you and Rani." He tousled my hair with a big leathery paw. I turned and headed through the gate. Mum would kill me for being so late. In the twilight, I put my shillings in my bank. They were the best shillings I had ever earned. They were the only shillings I had ever earned.

Next morning at school I felt like a prisoner.

I needed to escape to see Rani for one last time. We could hear the sound of diesel vehicles starting and revving and getting ready to go. Most of the circus had been dismantled and packed away into the wee hours after last night's performance.

"Miss Quinn – I don't think Spot looks too well. Can I take him out for five minutes?"

Miss Quinn looked at me and looked at Spot. Spot was looking a bit grey, lying on the floorboards and breathing lightly, totally out of it. Miss Quinn slowly reached for Spot's lead, hanging on the back of a chair, still suspiciously eying me up. No one else in Pomeroy had a lead for their dog.

"Alright Eamon. Give him a breath of fresh air for five minutes."

I took the lead and attached it to the leather collar around Spot's neck. He got up instantly. There was nothing wrong with him. I walked through the classroom door down the hall and opened the big front door. Spot obediently followed. I closed the door.

The playground was completely silent and empty. I wasn't used to that. I tied Spot's lead to the boy's metal mud remover down beside the front step. I stroked Spot behind the ear.

"You are on guard-dog duty for five minutes Spot, but no barking until I get back." I needn't have worried. Spot never barked at anything.

I sprinted to the edge of the playground and turned left down into Main Street. I was just in time. I hadn't missed the convoy leaving. I popped into Jo Hagan's.

"Hello Joe. I need a yellow bon-bon."

"What are you doin' out of school?" he asked as he reached for the large sweet jar containing the round yellow sweets.

"Just out for five minutes Joe or maybe ten."

"Well here – you might need this as well." He handed me one of those Sherbet Fountain packets that he knew was my favourite because it had liquorice in it. I grabbed the bon-bon and pocketed it and held tight to the packet of sherbet.

"You're lucky I have anything to give you. One of the circus monkeys got in here the other day and caused a bit of a furore. They had to fetch a net to catch the little blighter."

"You'll have met Sam then." I said

"The circus fella who looks like he should be on a pirate ship in the Caribbean?"

"That's him. He's the elephant trainer." I replied.

"And he's good at catchin' monkeys."

"I need to get going. Thanks for the sweets Joe, see you later!"

I walked out of the shop and paced a few yards to the right so I was standing directly in front of the Grotto. I had timed it perfectly. The first vehicles of the convoy had already passed, but they were travelling fairly slowly. There was a smell of diesel smoke and animals in the air. I opened my Sherbet Fountain and some of the precious white sherbet powder spilled out onto my white Aran jumper. I brushed it away and then paused.

Over the brow of Main Street I spotted the unmistakeable shape of an Elephant's head, coming into full view as Rani approached my da's garage. She was walking at a normal pace, led by Sam, wearing a black cowboy hat, the kind Jesse James wore in the westerns. I noticed a man in a dark overcoat just up ahead of me with a camera dangling from his neck who was shaping to take some photographs of the rare scene.

A few young boys who I didn't recognise were running behind. They must have been circus boys getting exercise too because they should have been at school, like me. Sam saw me as he approached and winked at me. Rani was almost opposite me now.

"Goodbye Rani!" I shouted at the top of my voice.

She turned her head slightly and caught me out of the side of her eye, raising her trunk and letting out a proper elephant's bellow. The noise reverberated off the painted plaster fronts of the houses on Main Street. The circus boys all stopped and looked at me. Sam theatrically raised his hat and gave a flourish and a bow in my direction. Rani ambled past and headed down the hill out of Pomeroy forever. I returned to my sherbet and liquorice. I would miss my elephant.

Two minutes later I was back at the front door of the school, slightly out of breath, with Spot was waiting faithfully, not that he had a choice in the matter. I patted the tight fur on the top of his head as a gesture of thanks and brought out the sweet from my pocket. Spot gobbled the yellow bon-bon in an instant. I unfastened the lead and took him back into the classroom. Miss Quinn never said a word and continued her lesson. Spot was lookin' great. I squeezed back into the double desk beside Adrian Nugent and he asked me what I'd been up to. I whispered to him that I had to see a man about an elephant. He looked at me like I was nuts. I would fill him in about Rani at breaktime.

It might have been the circus that distracted me but I hadn't been sleeping very well for a few nights. That night was the same. I told Mum the next morning and she took a good look at me.

"When I go to bed I can't sleep," I said.

Mum told me that I should just close my eyes and relax that night and not worry about anything.

"Will it be all right if I do that?" I asked.

"It will," she replied.

But that night was the same, another fitful night's sleep and I felt quite tired the next day. Mum was becoming concerned and took a closer look at me.

"What are those bruises on your legs?" she asked.

I hadn't noticed any bruises up to that point. I hadn't been playing football for the last few days or jumping over things or climbing stuff as I was concentrating on the circus and my elephant. Mum thought it might have been from the big bicycle that I had conquered but I knew it wasn't that. Mum told me to rest a while in bed and she went downstairs to make a phone call. Whatever she said, within half an hour our family doctor was by my bedside.

"How are you feeling Eamon?" asked Dr Meehan.

"Fine Doctor." I always wondered why you had to say Doctor instead of just saying their name. You didn't go up to a priest and say "hello Priest", or "see ya Teacher" to a teacher, or "Breadman give us some bread", or "Coalman where's my coal", unless his surname was actually Coleman. But with doctors you had to go yes Doctor, no Doctor, three bags full Doctor instead of "I'm doin' great Jimmy or whatever your name is". Doctors weren't called Jimmy though. You didn't know what they were called because everyone called them Doctor.

Doctor Meehan examined the bruises on my legs and did the usual stuff with the stethoscope and stuck a thermometer in my gob and asked me a few questions about how I was feeling. Then he took Mum outside the bedroom door and started murmuring about something. He left shortly afterwards. Mum looked a bit serious when she came back into the bedroom.

"You are going on a wee visit to hospital just to check out your bruises."

Mum wasted no time. I was in the car within half an hour and on my way to Dungannon hospital, which had been recently completed. At six storeys high, with a wee bit of seven stories, it was the tallest building by far in the town and it was positioned on one of the highest bits of the town, at the top of Quarry Lane. It almost felt too big for the town but maybe there were a lot of sick people in Dungannon. Dr Meehan had called ahead and there was a small welcoming party in white coats awaiting my arrival. They turned and guided me into the hospital foyer and straight over to a lift. It was my first time in a hospital apart from when I was born. Someone had been going bananas with the disinfectant in here. The smell was something else.

About seven years later, my wee brother Brendan would experience something similar with an unexpected visit to the same hospital.

He had been complaining about chest pains and I suppose Mum was taking no chances after what happened to me. And maybe because of what happened to me she didn't want to alarm him. She told Brendan that he was allowed to stay up late on a school night to visit some of his cousins from Dungannon who were in hospital. Brendan was quite excited, especially when Enda got packed off to bed with his tail between his legs. Again, there was a welcoming committee awaiting Brendan when he arrived but for some reason they put him on a trolley and wheeled him to a ward. At some point Brendan remembered that he was supposed to be here to visit cousins, a visitor and not a patient, so he asked Mum where they were. Mum told him to wave at his cousins as he went past. One of the Kellys, our first cousin, happened to be in the ward that the trolley went past at that time, wheeling towards its destination with an uncertain passenger, and Brendan realised that he had been classically duped again by his dear mother. He was in there for a week and they found nothing wrong with him, but they had to practically strap him to the bed when Mum left after visiting hour each day with him screaming the place down because he just wanted to get home. At least he was consistent. Mum should have given him some brandy and port and he'd be singin' himself and a man named Brown to sleep.

I was to stay just two nights on this first visit, so that they could carry out some tests. That didn't bother me at all.

I was placed on a ward with five other children. There were six beds in each ward with a curtain around your bed and everything. There were plugs everywhere and no carpets on the floor, just shiny green lino that looked clean enough to eat your breakfast off.

The other boys eyed me suspiciously as Mum put my stuff down on the bed. I was able to wear my own clothes so I didn't look like an escapee from the mental hospital with a medical smock open at the back. Mum lingered around for a bit but I told her not to worry. I knew I had a lot to explore in this massive building. As soon as she was gone, I pulled the curtain around the bed and stuck the pillow under the covers so that at a casual glance, it would look like I was sleeping underneath the bedclothes.

The bed was a bit odd. You had to jump a bit to get onto it and it was made out of tubular metal and had a medical note board hanging on the bars at the end of the bed. And it was on wheels and each wheel had its own brake. I could have some fun with that, I thought. There were hardly any covers compared to my bed at home, but the ward was quite warm and my fellow inmates were all in short sleeves.

I made a bee-line for the lifts. There was a staircase to the side of the lift so I used that to explore what was above me and what was below. From the stair landing I could see my floor was about five storeys up with a view over the roofs of all the terraced houses in the part of town called the White City. To the right, I could see the roof of the Technical College. The floors above and below were identical to mine, just with adults instead of children.

I went back to my floor and investigated that. It was mostly made up of open wards but there were a few private rooms at the end and there was a counter near the lifts with a load of nurses hangin' around it looking at paperwork or answering the phone.

I went to the wall-to-wall window at the end of my ward. You could see into the centre of Dungannon from here and I could just make out the blue and white Ulsterbuses turning in The Square, the centre of the town in front of Wellworth's store. Beyond the top of the Square was the old castle of Hugh O'Neill. This is where the last Celtic chieftain of Ulster had ruled from. There wasn't much left of his command post.

"What are ye in for?" The boy nearest the window asked me. He was a bit older than me but looked friendly enough.

"Bad behaviour."

"What did you do?"

"I chased an elephant out of our town."

"You did what?"

I heard some serious sounding adults speaking behind me. I turned around. More white coats were hangin' around my bed. I'd forgotten to take the pillow out so I had to improvise.

"Just keepin' my pillow warm," I said as I squeezed between the white coats and straightened up my bed. I climbed onto it and awaited their questions.

They asked me to lie down on the bed. They started doing all sorts of tests on me. Blood pressure, heart rate, blood tests and lots of questions that I'd already answered to Dr Meehan. I was wearing short trousers so I didn't have the embarrassment of taking my clothes off in front of them, just my t-shirt. One of the white coats was black. He was the first black man I had ever met. I'd seen loads in the Tarzan movies but they looked different in the flesh. This man was tall and looked far healthier than the other white coats. He saw me staring at him and smiled. I put my hand out and said.

"Wee lad from Pomeroy."

"Kojo," he said.

"Pleased to meet you." I stopped staring at him. He was cool. He didn't need to be called 'Doctor'.

They fussed over me for another half an hour, made a load of notes on the board at the end of my bed and then left me in peace. Mum visited me in the evening. By that time I had gotten to know the other kids on the ward and one or two of the kids in the other wards on the floor. They were from Dungannnon and Coalisland mainly with someone from Moygashel which is where the Protestants lived. I was the only one from Pomeroy. The funny thing was, none of the children looked ill enough to be in hospital apart for the Moygashel boy whose leg was strapped to the ceiling and he wasn't able to move. The eejit had fallen out of a tree when he was trying to mess up a bird's nest.

Mum came and collected me on the third morning but she didn't look happy.

Unbeknown to me the doctors had just told her that I had six months to live.

One of the nurses was called Molly, and Molly had told Mum that morning to spend as much time with me as she could and take the good of me while she had me.

Mum never told me this at the time but I knew something was wrong. I didn't realise it but my body was slowly deteriorating and there was no cure for what I had.

I also hadn't realised it but I had spent my last day at school. Mum had spoken to Master Anderson and that was that. I should have been over the moon but I knew I would miss my friends and Miss Quinn and Spot and warm school milk and the noise of the playground and running around like mad things and the stories about CúChulainn and the Red Branch Knights. I'd even miss that old books smell of the classroom. Mum and I were going to spend as much time together in the time that I had left. We visited all the Canavan and Farrell relatives in Ballygawley and the McGirrs and Kellys as well and Mum's three sisters in Dungannon and Mum's cousin Braid Quinn in Aughnacloy.

She kept me supplied with Brandy Ball sweets and chewy Drumsticks. She showed me how to make wheaten bread and told me that people in the Free State called it soda bread, but we knew that soda bread was white, not brown and she showed me how to make that too, on her big black heavy frying pan. She offered to show me how to darn socks but that was going too far for me. I had my street credibility to think of.

My First Holy Communion was fast-tracked which was brilliant. I was kitted out with new clothes for the big day. No hand-me-downs from Aidan and Kieran on this occasion. New shoes as well. As I walked up the central aisle of the chapel there was a little smirk on my face. My classmates were on either side of me, boys on the right and girls on the left, looking on in total jealousy as these eejits wouldn't be taking this walk for at least another year.

Father McKeown was on duty that day and he winked at me as he put the communion host on my tongue.

Forty years later, in a little French chapel over three thousand miles away in Monfort, deep in the Canadian province of Quebec, Brendan's son Edward was within a few weeks of having received his First Holy Communion. The experience was a little different for young Ed. For a start, the mass was in French and on top of that one of the hymns was the same as the theme tune for the movie, Dr Zhivago. You didn't get that in Weybridge England where he grew up. He received

138

the host into his hand from the French Canadian priest but the host was different from what he was used to as the little circular disc was made from wholemeal, with flecks of grain, instead of being like the pure white wafers in England. Brendan noticed that Edward had returned to his seat without consuming the precious host. He whispered urgently.

"What are you doing Edward? Eat the Communion!"

"I can't, it's got germs on it!" Edward responded.

"How can the body of Christ have germs on it? Eat it now!"

Edward reluctantly complied and put the host in his mouth.

He and his little brother Oscar would be humming the Dr Zhivago theme music for weeks afterwards.

I had many visits from doctors over the next few months, checking up on me.

The school sent me up a tiny blackboard attached to a string and some chalk so I could carry on learning or drawing. I drew a flag on the blackboard. It was the same flag I always drew, the Irish flag. I had to draw the green as white with my stick of chalk and the orange as white too, but slightly less white and the white bit in the middle was black, the colour of the blackboard. But there was no mistaking the drawing. This was the Irish Tricolour.

I began to notice that Mum would erase the drawing of the flag just before some of the doctors arrived. After about the third time that she had done this I was beginning to get annoyed so I asked her.

"Mum, why do you keep rubbing out my wee flag?"

"Well Eamon, the doctor who is visiting you today is a Protestant doctor and he doesn't believe in the Irish flag. The Union Jack is his flag."

I was perplexed.

"So why don't we put the two together?" I asked putting the palms of my hands outwards in a conciliatory gesture and then reaching for the chalk. Mum smiled as broadly as I had seen her smile since before my first hospital visit. She maybe thought that the doctor wouldn't have treated me as well if I was showing signs of Irish nationalism by my bedhead. I didn't really get it though. We had been taught at school that the Irish flag represented everyone. The green represented the original Irish, largely Catholic people of Ireland. The orange represented the Protestant people of Ireland and was clear recognition of William of Orange, or King Billy as everyone called him in the North and the white bit in the middle represented peace between the people of Ireland. A flag that said all that should be good enough for everybody I thought.

A little later, I went downstairs and Mum roped me into helping her polish the silverware with Silvo and a cloth rag in the dining room. Kieran and Aidan were watching TV in the front room.

I had decided that if I was going to go to Heaven I might as well do it properly. After all, Ireland was a Land of Saints and Scholars. It was almost the first thing you learned at school. Ireland had saved the world from a total collapse into barbarism. After the fall of the Roman Empire, Christianity had spread throughout Ireland and we began spreading it back to Scotland and northern England. Ireland was the first country to send the Vikings packing, in 1014 at the Battle of Clontarf with Brian Boru, the High King of Ireland, leading the rout. Then, in the dark ages, we had sent out monks across Europe to keep the small fires of civilization alight. And today we were still going strong sending missionaries out to Calcutta and Jonestown, where Aunty Clare was stationed and elsewhere to save the world again and make sure people blessed themselves with their right hand instead of their left.

"What would I need to do to be a saint?" I asked her.

"Well, you would need to behave, be kind to everyone and not fight with your brothers and say lots of prayers and forgive people who aren't so nice to you."

"That sounds hard," I responded.

Mum grabbed an edition of Africa magazine.

"Funnily enough there's the story of a young saint in here."

She told me the story of Dominic Saveo. He had died in northern Italy in 1857 when he was just fourteen, of pleurisy or something like that. He was the son of a blacksmith so he was from a fairly poor background and he was studying to be a priest. He is the youngest saint in the Catholic Church to have died naturally and not having been killed for his faith. Africa magazine was a missionary pamphlet that got delivered periodically to our house along with Time magazine. I preferred Time magazine because it had wee diagrams telling you how many tanks, planes and ICBMs NATO had compared to the Russians and it didn't have any holy stuff in it at all.

"What's pleurisy?" I asked.

"A type of lung infection."

"So why did they make him a saint?"

"Because he led such a holy life. He was very bright but he was an ordinary boy He enjoyed playing as well as school, and he must have liked school because he trudged twelve miles there and back every day and he could control his emotions so that he wouldn't get angry."

"Did he have any shoes on his feet?" This was an in-joke as Mum had told me once that she used to walk to school in Glencull barefoot in the early summer and I had this image in my mind of my mum as a shoeless urchin.

"I think he had shoes on," she laughed.

"What did he look like?"

"A wee bit like you."

I smiled.

"Why don't we both try our best to be saints?" she suggested.

"Let's try," I said. "You point out my faults and I'll point out yours."

We finished polishing the silverware and put it back on the big dark wooden sideboard at the edge of the dining room. Mum pulled out a sweet, a humbug, from a pocket of her cardigan and gave it to me.

"What do you say?"

"Have you got any more?" I asked. I knew Curly wanted one.

"Not quite the answer I was expecting." Mum smiled and produced another sweet.

We could hear a bit of a commotion from the living room. The twins were fighting again. Mum walked across the hall and opened the living room door and started bellowing at them to stop their scrapping.

She came back into the dining room looking a little flustered.

"You'll never be a saint shouting at them like that," I told her.

Now she smiled again.

141

"You're right there Eamon."

I had another spell in hospital for further tests.

After a few days' time I had amassed a significant collection of sweets, biscuits and fruit.

Loads of people came to visit me and my Aunty Betty and Aunty Celine were never out of the place. My Aunty Mena was a nurse so she came a calling any time she liked. Aunties were better at visiting than uncles, except for Uncle Jim who was married to Mum's sister Betty, and he always had his camera with him. He was in one day when Mum and Dad were in as well and took a few photographs of us. Uncle Jim made Mum and Dad sit on the hospital bed beside me so he could get a good shot. I was a bit embarrassed to have my parents piling onto the bed with the other hungry lads on the ward, without a parent between them by the look of it, gawping at me. I grabbed my Thunderbirds pistol so I could look cool no matter what. Uncle Jim said he'd develop the photographs and come back in to show me in a few days' time.

Father McDermott even came in to see me, in his wheelchair. I greeted him at the entrance to the ward and clambered up the left hand wheel so I could get a lift back to my bed. He didn't stay long as Kathleen was fussing over him but I appreciated the visit from the old priest.

I had asked Mum to bring in a big cardboard box to keep all my stuff in and I began to sell some of it to those less well-off and clearly hungry children. I kept the box under my bed so it was fairly safe. A boy called George on the opposite side of the ward, two beds down, was always eyeing up the box and sniffing around expecting something. I asked Mum to bring in a good thief-proof lid for the box. She brought in a cardboard lid and some string the next day.

Just after she arrived I got her help on something.

"Take the box over to that brown haired lad over there and sell him whatever it is he's after. But keep a close eye on him 'cos I don't trust him." George heard me and smiled back over at me. He knew I was only half serious. Mum dutifully obliged and George got what he wanted, a box of Dolly Mixture sweets and forked out the money, with me watching every twitch and nervous flick as he made his selection, from the comfort of my bed.

I started to rent out the toys that people brought me to the other boys on the ward and in other wards too. The going rate was a penny an hour. By the time I came out of hospital I had saved fourteen pounds. This was enough savings to buy a second-hand car and I had more money in my Bank. Mum would be thrilled. I didn't mind my time in hospital. It was a good place to do business and the days flew by. I suppose I slept for a good part of the day but I was still full of beans when awake.

I spent my last month at home.

People sometimes talk about battling a disease or illness. This was no battle. This was a full-scale invasion and the defending army was being decimated. You can't fight a battle if you don't have any weapons. I was defenceless.

Mum moved me into her and Dad's bedroom at the front of the house. I supposed that this was to allow visitors easier access and movement in a bigger bedroom and there were many visitors.

I gradually ran out of energy and had to spend more time in bed or on the sofa in the front room watching TV. Kieran and Aidan gave me first choice of television watching, which was highly unusual. A brand new series of Batman had just come out and I wouldn't miss an episode. Batman had been strictly confined to the DC comics up until then and now here he was in full technicolour. Batman and Robin came perilously close in every episode to meeting a grisly death at the hands of The Joker or The Riddler but always ended up saving the day.

Kieran was particularly attentive when he got home at weekends. He had gotten his Eleven Plus a year early and had gone off to boarding school in Armagh, leaving his twin behind. He was away for a lot of my last six months but I could tell that he wished he was here. The Armagh College thing was a Kilpatrick tradition. All the boys went there. The tradition would be broken by Brendan who, typically, refused to go to a place which was so far from home.

My friend Adrian visited me almost every day and kept me up to date with what was happening in the classroom and the playground. In my last week or so, Adrian went home and told his mum that I wasn't very well. He knew the end was close. Dad needed to carry me up from the sofa after watching TV.

Mum looked after me and made me comfortable. Doctors came and went. Nurse Molly visited. My school chums visited. Everyone visited. Even Father McDermott came, abandoning his wheelchair and ascending the staircase like he was climbing Mount Everest to visit me for one last time.

"I look better than you do," I said as he emerged breathless into the bedroom, assisted by Kathleen.

"I've brought you some chocolate," he said as produced a bar of Fry's Chocolate Cream. I still had the taste for it.

Many of the visits were a bit of a blur and I wasn't as talkative as I wanted to be, but I wasn't in any pain.

"What can I get you Eamon?" Mum asked in those last few days.

"I've got everything I need," I answered. My only regret was that I hadn't managed to get Mum that car. Dad would have to take care of that. I made sure she knew where my money was hidden.

As my energy dropped, I cared less about my physical wellbeing and trusted in Mum and her prayers. I began to realise that I would soon be joining my big sister Maeve but it didn't worry me. I knew that I had squeezed an awful lot into the last few years and had seen what I needed to see. I had travelled around the place more than many adults in the village and had gotten to know loads of people. I never felt sad because I knew I would somehow stay in touch with my family, even Brendan and Enda. I was glad I hadn't sold Enda now. He was squawking a lot less as he was getting older. Plus I knew that Curly would be coming with me. There was no ban on ginger hair where I was going.

And I was glad I was at home.

My last evening was a drowsy episode as I drifted in and out of consciousness and then out for the last time; shortly after that, on the fifth of March 1967, my heart beat its last.

For a decade and a half after, Mum launched herself into raising funds for leukaemia research. In true Canavan style, she was determined to snatch some form of victory from the dodgy hand she had been dealt. Her five remaining sons were roped into this new cause, selling tickets, collecting for raffle prizes, and attending fund-raising fetes and functions. She would be relentless in her dedication to the cause of eradicating the

disease that had taken me from her. She would receive generous and continuous support in her mission from friends and family, and in particular from the people of Pomeroy, many of whom I had come across casually or gone to school with or travelled across the North with or simply invaded their territory unannounced.

The two nights of the funeral wake saw the house packed out. A legion of relatives descended upon the house to help Mum with the tea and sandwiches, while the publicans in the village supplied enough booze to keep the late night watchers lubricated. It was a sad wake because of my youth but Mum was warmed by the tales about me that she heard over these few days and in the time after the funeral, stories which helped keep her sadness contained. Kieran and Aidan were devastated to have lost their wee brother and were old enough to feel the pain of loss. Brendan and Enda hadn't a clue what was going on and were packed off to Kathleen next door in the Parochial House.

The funeral that took place on the third day was huge, completely filling the church, with additional mourners hanging around outside the entrance doors as there was no room to get in. It was one of the biggest funerals the village had seen. Not bad for a six year old. The funeral mass was conducted by the man who had given me my First Holy Communion just a few months before, Father McKeown. He wasn't winking now and, in truth, the funeral mass was a sombre affair with my small coffin at the head of the central aisle in front of the altar. He spoke about me as someone who knew me and this gave Mum and Dad some comfort.

There were more people around the graveside than there were at Maeve's, but then I had a good six years over her, and here I was heading into the same spot as my wee sister. It hadn't occurred to me that we'd be sharing a grave.

Mum stood by the grave's opening. Dad was at her side. Kieran and Aidan were standing in front of them wiping tears from their eyes. Mum didn't cry. She hadn't shed a single tear in the whole funeral proceedings. Not that this was easy for her. She didn't cry because she knew that I was up there with the saints.

And I suppose I am.

The struggle to cure childhood leukaemia was a massive undertaking over many decades.

Less than four years after I had gone and just eight years into his tenure at St. Jude, Don Pinkel was able to make an extraordinary pronouncement. It was 1970 when he said, "Childhood leukaemia can no longer be considered an incurable disease." The hospital was seeing a 50 per cent cure rate.

This of course was four years too late for me and in reality more like a decade too late by the time that Europe had caught up medically with the United States.

Today, building on protocols he and his staff established at St. Jude, the survival rate for most forms of childhood leukaemia hovers around 85 percent. In reality I was knocking around about ten years too early for Doctor Pinkel to save me. Or should I say Don?

After publishing his findings and consolidating his breakthroughs at St. Jude, Don Pinkel soon considered a change in direction. In 1974, he resigned as the hospital's director and took a series of eminent hospital and faculty posts, helping to establish new faculties before moving on to the next challenge.

His approach to total therapy is still being used to this day.